MW00422912

Rape and Dating Violence

**Recent Titles in
Q&A Health Guides**

Teen Stress: Your Questions Answered
Nicole Neda Zamanzadeh and Tamara D. Afifi

Grief and Loss: Your Questions Answered
Louis Kuykendall Jr.

Healthy Friendships: Your Questions Answered
Lauren Holleb

Trauma and Resilience: Your Questions Answered
Keith A. Young

Vegetarian and Vegan Diets: Your Questions Answered
Alice C. Richer

Yoga: Your Questions Answered
Anjali A. Sarkar

Teen Pregnancy: Your Questions Answered
Paul Quinn

Sexual Harassment: Your Questions Answered
Justine J. Reel

Sports Injuries: Your Questions Answered
James H. Johnson

Essential Oils: Your Questions Answered
Randi Minetor

Hormones: Your Questions Answered
Tish Davidson

Marijuana: Your Questions Answered
Aharon W. Zorea

Exercise: Your Questions Answered
Justine J. Reel

Acne: Your Questions Answered
Shayan Waseh

RAPE AND DATING VIOLENCE

Your Questions Answered

Lee Ann Ritscher

Q&A Health Guides

GREENWOOD

An Imprint of ABC-CLIO, LLC
Santa Barbara, California • Denver, Colorado

Library of Congress Cataloging-in-Publication Data

Names: Ritscher, Lee A., 1961- author.
Title: Rape and dating violence : your questions answered / Lee Ann
   Ritscher.
Description: Santa Barbara, California : Greenwood, [2023] | Series: Q&A
   health guides | Includes bibliographical references and index.
Identifiers: LCCN 2022029878 | ISBN 9781440867675 (print) | ISBN
   9781440867682 (ebook)
Subjects: LCSH: Rape. | Sex crimes. | Dating violence.
Classification: LCC HV6558 .R58 2023 | DDC 362.88392—dc23/eng/20221021
LC record available at https://lccn.loc.gov/2022029878

ISBN: 978-1-4408-6767-5 (print)
         978-1-4408-6768-2 (ebook)

27 26 25 24 23   1 2 3 4 5

This book is also available as an eBook.

Greenwood
An Imprint of ABC-CLIO, LLC

ABC-CLIO, LLC
147 Castilian Drive
Santa Barbara, California 93117
www.abc-clio.com

This book is printed on acid-free paper ∞

Manufactured in the United States of America

This book is dedicated to all my family members for their support and encouragement during the writing of this book, but in particular to my mother, Ann Wright, and my husband, Paul Ritscher—without you two, this would not have been possible. This book is also dedicated to the men and women I have known who have suffered dating or domestic violence, sexual abuse, sexual assault, or rape. I hope this book answers some of your questions or helps you figure out how to have healthy relationships. Every one of us deserves that.

Contents

Series Foreword   xi

Introduction   xiii

Guide to Health Literacy   xv

Common Misconceptions about Rape and Dating Violence   xxiii

Questions and Answers   1

The Basics   3

   1. What is dating violence?   3
   2. How common is dating violence in the United States and
      who is most likely to experience it?   6
   3. What are the signs of dating violence?   8
   4. What is consent and why does it matter?   10
   5. How should consent be asked for and given?   12
   6. What is rape?   13
   7. What is statutory rape?   15
   8. What is the difference between rape, sexual assault, and
      sexual abuse?   17
   9. How common is rape in the United States and who is
      most likely to become a victim of rape or sexual assault?   18
  10. What are the signs of rape?   21

11. How common are rape and dating violence
    around the world?   23
12. What is stalking? What is cyberstalking?   26
13. How common are false charges of rape and
    dating violence?   27

Causes, Consequences, and Prevention of Rape and
Dating Violence   31

14. What causes dating violence?   31
15. What causes rape?   34
16. What is the cycle of abuse?   37
17. What are the short- and long-term physical
    consequences of dating violence?   39
18. What are the short- and long-term physical
    consequences of rape?   41
19. What happens if a woman becomes pregnant
    as a result of rape?   43
20. What are the long-term psychological effects for
    victims of rape or dating violence?   46
21. What is PTSD?   48
22. What are the psychological impacts for those who
    perpetrate rape, sexual assault, or dating violence?   51
23. What are the legal consequences for perpetrators of
    rape, sexual assault, and dating violence?   53
24. What are Romeo and Juliet laws?   55
25. What is the sex offender list and how does
    someone get on it?   57
26. How can being convicted of rape or sexual assault
    impact someone's life?   58
27. How can rape and dating violence be prevented?   60
28. Is there anything individuals can do to help minimize
    their chances of becoming a victim of rape or
    dating violence?   63
29. Is it possible to completely eliminate rape and
    dating violence in the future?   64

Seeking Help   67

30. What services are available for victims of rape and
    sexual assault?   67
31. What services are available for victims of
    dating violence?   69

32. What should I do or not do immediately
    following a rape?   73
33. I think I may have been raped, but I'm not sure.
    What should I do?   74
34. I think I may have crossed a line during sex and
    am worried that what I did could be considered rape.
    What should I do?   76
35. I think I've committed dating violence.
    What should I do?   78
36. I am in a sexual relationship with someone older or
    younger than me and am worried about accusations of
    statutory rape. What should I do?   79
37. If I seek medical help or counseling for rape or dating
    violence, do I have to report the incident to the police?
    Are those helping me required to report the
    incident to the police?   81
38. Should I get a restraining order? How do I get one?   82

Rape, Dating Violence, and Culture   85

39. How does the media impact our perceptions of
    rape and dating violence?   85
40. What is rape culture?   87
41. What is victim blaming?   89
42. What is the #MeToo movement about?   91
43. What is a SlutWalk? How do I start one?   93

Case Studies   97

Glossary   113
Directory of Resources   117
Index   123

Series Foreword

All of us have questions about our health. Is this normal? Should I be doing something differently? Whom should I talk to about my concerns? And our modern world is full of answers. Thanks to the Internet, there's a wealth of information at our fingertips, from forums where people can share their personal experiences to Wikipedia articles to the full text of medical studies. But finding the right information can be an intimidating and difficult task—some sources are written at too high a level, others have been oversimplified, while still others are heavily biased or simply inaccurate.

Q&A Health Guides address the needs of readers who want accurate, concise answers to their health questions, authored by reputable and objective experts, and written in clear and easy-to-understand language. This series focuses on the topics that matter most to young adult readers, including various aspects of physical and emotional well-being as well as other components of a healthy lifestyle. These guides will also serve as a valuable tool for parents, school counselors, and others who may need to answer teens' health questions.

All books in the series follow the same format to make finding information quick and easy. Each volume begins with an essay on health literacy and why it is so important when it comes to gathering and evaluating health information. Next, the top five myths and misconceptions that surround the topic are dispelled. The heart of each guide is a collection of questions and answers, organized thematically. A selection of five case studies provides real-world examples to illuminate key concepts. Rounding out each volume are a directory of resources, glossary, and index.

It is our hope that the books in this series will not only provide valuable information but will also help guide readers toward a lifetime of healthy decision making.

Introduction

The fact that one in every six women will experience rape in their life-time is rationale for any book about the topic. While statistically speaking few of these rapes will be prosecuted, people who find themselves in this situation have long needed a book that addresses their experience in a straightforward, easy-to-understand manner. This book is primarily aimed at those who are at an age when they are more likely to have this trau-matic experience than at any other time in their lives—people in their late teens and early twenties. While some people go through life without having an experience of sexual assault, rape, or dating or domestic vio-lence, there are enough of us out there that a book that seeks to answer our questions makes a lot of sense.

This book is aimed at young adults who are just beginning intimate relationships and need some guidance in how to form mutually satisfying relationships that respect the needs of each partner. Our culture does a pretty poor job of providing guidance on this topic, and this book hopes to provide some of that guidance. In addition to rape and sexual assault, this book also looks at dating and domestic violence, as they are also com-mon in our culture, and it looks at how rape culture perpetuates gen-dered stereotypes that hurt everyone—male, female, cisgender, trans, and LGBTQIA+.

This book was created during the #MeToo era, and the interest in hold-ing people accountable for their sexual assaults and rapes does not seem to have waned in the intervening time period. In fact, there seems to be more interest than ever, as many schools have returned to holding Slut-Walks and performances of *The Vagina Monologues* and inviting others to participate in this creation of a culture that sees sexual assault, rape, and dating and domestic violence as unacceptable elements in our society. The more that these sorts of movements create that culture, the fewer of us who will have to endure these experiences.

Guide to Health Literacy

On her 13th birthday, Samantha was diagnosed with type 2 diabetes. She consulted her mom and her aunt, both of whom also have type 2 diabetes, and decided to go with their strategy of managing diabetes by taking insulin. As a result of participating in an after-school program at her middle school that focused on health literacy, she learned that she can help manage the level of glucose in her bloodstream by counting her carbohydrate intake, following a diabetic diet, and exercising regularly. But, what exactly should she do? How does she keep track of her carbohydrate intake? What is a diabetic diet? How long should she exercise and what type of exercise should she do? Samantha is a visual learner, so she turned to her favorite source of media, YouTube, to answer these questions. She found videos from individuals around the world sharing their experiences and tips, doctors (or at least people who have "Dr." in their YouTube channel names), government agencies such as the National Institutes of Health, and even video clips from cat lovers who have cats with diabetes. With guidance from the librarian and the health and science teachers at her school, she assessed the credibility of the information in these videos and even compared their suggestions to some of the print resources that she was able to find at her school library. Now, she knows exactly how to count her carbohydrate level, how to prepare and follow a diabetic diet, and how much (and what) exercise is needed daily. She intends to share her findings with her mom and her aunt, and now she wants to create a chart that summarizes what she has learned that she can share with her doctor.

Samantha's experience is not unique. She represents a shift in our society; an individual no longer views himself or herself as a passive recipient of medical care but as an active mediator of his or her own health. However, in this era when any individual can post his or her opinions and experiences with a particular health condition online with just a few clicks or publish a memoir, it is vital that people know how to assess the credibility of health information. Gone are the days when "publishing" health information required intense vetting. The health information landscape is highly saturated, and people have innumerable sources where they can find information about practically any health topic. The sources (whether print, online, or a person) that an individual consults for health information are crucial because the accuracy and trustworthiness of the information can potentially affect his or her overall health. The ability to find, select, assess, and use health information constitutes a type of literacy—health literacy—that everyone must possess.

THE DEFINITION AND PHASES OF HEALTH LITERACY

One of the most popular definitions for health literacy comes from Ratzan and Parker (2000), who describe health literacy as "the degree to which individuals have the capacity to obtain, process, and understand basic health information and services needed to make appropriate health decisions." Recent research has extrapolated health literacy into health literacy bits, further shedding light on the multiple phases and literacy practices that are embedded within the multifaceted concept of health literacy. Although this research has focused primarily on online health information seeking, these health literacy bits are needed to successfully navigate both print and online sources. There are six phases of health information seeking: (1) Information Need Identification and Question Formulation, (2) Information Search, (3) Information Comprehension, (4) Information Assessment, (5) Information Management, and (6) Information Use.

The first phase is the *information need identification and question formulation phase*. In this phase, one needs to be able to develop and refine a range of questions to frame one's search and understand relevant health terms. In the second phase, *information search*, one has to possess appropriate searching skills, such as using proper keywords and correct spelling in search terms, especially when using search engines and databases. It is also crucial to understand how search engines work (i.e., how search results are derived, what the order of the search results means, how to use the snippets that are provided in the search results list to select websites, and how to determine which listings are ads on a search engine results page). One also has to limit reliance on surface characteristics, such as the design of a website or a book (a website or book that appears to have a lot of information or looks aesthetically pleasant does not necessarily mean it has good information) and language used (a website or book that utilizes jargon, the keywords that one used to conduct the search, or the word "information" does not necessarily indicate it will have good information). The next phase is *information comprehension*, whereby one needs to have the ability to read, comprehend, and recall the information (including textual, numerical, and visual content) one has located from the books and/or online resources.

To assess the credibility of health information (*information assessment* phase), one needs to be able to evaluate information for accuracy, evaluate how current the information is (e.g., when a website was last updated or when a book was published), and evaluate the creators of the source—for example, examine site sponsors or type of sites (.com, .gov, .edu, or .org) or the author of a book (practicing doctor, a celebrity doctor, a patient of a specific disease, etc.) to determine the believability of the person/organization providing the information. Such credibility perceptions tend to become generalized, so they must be frequently reexamined (e.g., the belief that a specific news agency always has credible health information needs continuous vetting). One also needs to evaluate the credibility of the medium (e.g., television, Internet, radio, social media, and book) and evaluate—not just accept without questioning—others' claims regarding the validity of a site, book, or other specific source of information. At this stage, one has to "make sense of information gathered from diverse sources by identifying misconceptions, main and supporting ideas, conflicting information, point of view, and biases" (American Association of School Librarians [AASL], 2009, p. 13) and conclude which sources/information are valid and accurate by using conscious strategies rather than simply using intuitive judgments or "rules of thumb." This phase is the most challenging segment of health information seeking and serves as a determinant of success (or lack thereof) in the information-seeking process. The following section on Sources of Health Information further explains this phase.

The fifth phase is *information management*, whereby one has to organize information that has been gathered in some manner to ensure easy retrieval and use in the future. The last phase is *information use*, in which one will synthesize information found across various resources, draw conclusions, and locate the answer to his or her original question and/ or the content that fulfills the information need. This phase also often involves implementation, such as using the information to solve a health problem; make health-related decisions; identify and engage in behaviors that will help a person to avoid health risks; share the health information found with family members and friends who may benefit from it; and advocate more broadly for personal, family, or community health.

THE IMPORTANCE OF HEALTH LITERACY

The conception of health has moved from a passive view (someone is either well or ill) to one that is more active and process based (someone is working toward preventing or managing disease). Hence, the dominant focus has shifted from doctors and treatments to patients and prevention, resulting in the need to strengthen our ability and confidence (as patients and consumers of health care) to look for, assess, understand, manage, share, adapt, and use health-related information. An individual's health literacy level has been found to predict his or her health status better than age, race, educational attainment, employment status, and income level (National Network of Libraries of Medicine, 2013). Greater health literacy also enables individuals to better communicate with health care providers such as doctors, nutritionists, and therapists, as they can pose more relevant, informed, and useful questions to health care providers. Another added advantage of greater health literacy is better information-seeking skills, not only for health but also in other domains, such as completing assignments for school.

SOURCES OF HEALTH INFORMATION: THE GOOD, THE BAD, AND THE IN-BETWEEN

For generations, doctors, nurses, nutritionists, health coaches, and other health professionals have been the trusted sources of health information. Additionally, researchers have found that young adults, when they have health-related questions, typically turn to a family member who has had firsthand experience with a health condition because of their family member's close proximity and because of their past experience with, and trust in, this individual. Expertise should be a core consideration when consulting a person, website, or book for health information. The credentials and background of the person or author and conflicting interests of the author (and his or her organization) must be checked and validated to ensure the likely credibility of the health information they are conveying. While books often have implied credibility because of the peer-review process involved, self-publishing has challenged this credibility, so qualifications of book authors should also be verified. When it comes to health information, currency of the source must also be examined. When examining health information/studies presented, pay attention to the exhaustiveness of research methods utilized to offer recommendations or conclusions. Small and nondiverse sample size is often—but not always—an indication of reduced credibility. Studies that confuse correlation with causation is another potential issue to watch for. Information seekers must also pay attention to the sponsors of the research studies. For example, if a study is sponsored by manufacturers of drug Y and the study recommends that drug Y is the best treatment to manage or cure a disease, this may indicate a lack of objectivity on the part of the researchers.

The Internet is rapidly becoming one of the main sources of health information. Online forums, news agencies, personal blogs, social media sites, pharmacy sites, and celebrity "doctors" are all offering medical and health information targeted to various types of people in regard to all types of diseases and symptoms. There are professional journalists, citizen journalists, hoaxers, and people paid to write fake health news on various sites that may appear to have a legitimate domain name and may even have authors who claim to have professional credentials, such as an MD. All these sites *may* offer useful information or information that appears to be useful and relevant; however, much of the information may be debatable and may fall into gray areas that require readers to discern credibility, reliability, and biases.

While broad recognition and acceptance of certain media, institutions, and people often serve as the most popular determining factors to assess credibility of health information among young people, keep in mind that there are legitimate Internet sites, databases, and books that publish health information and serve as sources of health information for doctors, other health sites, and members of the public. For example, MedlinePlus (https://medlineplus.gov) has trusted sources on over 975 diseases and conditions and presents the information in easy-to-understand language.

The chart here presents factors to consider when assessing credibility of health information. However, keep in mind that these factors function only as a guide and require continuous updating to keep abreast with the changes in the landscape of health information, information sources, and technologies.

The chart can serve as a guide; however, approaching a librarian about how one can go about assessing the credibility of both print and online health information is far more effective than using generic checklist-type

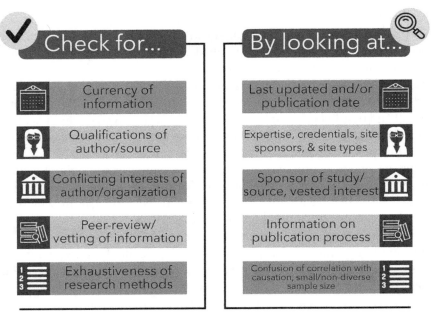

All images from flaticon.com

tools. While librarians are not health experts, they can apply and teach patrons strategies to determine the credibility of health information.

With the prevalence of fake sites and fake resources that appear to be legitimate, it is important to use the following health information assessment tips to verify health information that one has obtained (St. Jean et al., 2015, p. 151):

- **Don't assume you are right**: Even when you feel very sure about an answer, keep in mind that the answer may not be correct, and it is important to conduct (further) searches to validate the information.
- **Don't assume you are wrong**: You may actually have correct information, even if the information you encounter does not match—that is, you may be right and the resources that you have found may contain false information.
- **Take an open approach**: Maintain a critical stance by not including your preexisting beliefs as keywords (or letting them influence your choice of keywords) in a search, as this may influence what it is possible to find out.
- **Verify, verify, and verify**: Information found, especially on the Internet, needs to be validated, no matter how the information appears on

the site (i.e., regardless of the appearance of the site or the quantity of information that is included).

Health literacy comes with experience navigating health information. Professional sources of health information, such as doctors, health care providers, and health databases, are still the best, but one also has the power to search for health information and then verify it by consulting with these trusted sources and by using the health information assessment tips and guide shared previously.

Mega Subramaniam, PhD

Associate Professor, College of Information Studies,

University of Maryland

REFERENCES AND FURTHER READING

American Association of School Librarians (AASL). (2009). *Standards for the 21st-century learner in action*. Chicago, IL: American Association of School Librarians.

Hilligoss, B., & Rieh, S.-Y. (2008). Developing a unifying framework of credibility assessment: Construct, heuristics, and interaction in context. *Information Processing & Management, 44*(4), 1467–1484.

Kuhlthau, C. C. (1988). Developing a model of the library search process: Cognitive and affective aspects. *Reference Quarterly, 28*(2), 232–242.

National Network of Libraries of Medicine (NNLM). (2013). Health literacy. Bethesda, MD: National Network of Libraries of Medicine. Retrieved from nnlm.gov/outreach/consumer/hlthlit.html

Ratzan, S. C., & Parker, R. M. (2000). Introduction. In C. R. Selden, M. Zorn, S. C. Ratzan, & R. M. Parker (Eds.), *National Library of Medicine current bibliographies in medicine: Health literacy*. NLM Pub. No. CBM 2000-1. Bethesda, MD: National Institutes of Health, U.S. Department of Health and Human Services.

St. Jean, B., Taylor, N. G., Kodama, C., & Subramaniam, M. (February 2017). Assessing the health information source perceptions of tweens using card-sorting exercises. *Journal of Information Science*. Retrieved from http://journals.sagepub.com/doi/abs/10.1177/0165551516687728

St. Jean, B., Subramaniam, M., Taylor, N. G., Follman, R., Kodama, C., & Casciotti, D. (2015). The influence of positive hypothesis testing on youths' online health-related information seeking. *New Library World, 116*(3/4), 136–154.

Subramaniam, M., St. Jean, B., Taylor, N. G., Kodama, C., Follman, R., & Casciotti, D. (2015). Bit by bit: Using design-based research to improve the health literacy of adolescents. *JMIR Research Protocols*, 4(2), paper e62. Retrieved from http://www.ncbi.nlm.nih.gov/pmc/articles/PMC4464334/

Valenza, J. (2016, November 26). Truth, truthiness, and triangulation: A news literacy toolkit for a "post-truth" world [Web log]. Retrieved from http://blogs.slj.com/neverendingsearch/2016/11/26/truth-truthiness-triangulation-and-the-librarian-way-a-news-literacy-toolkit-for-a-post-truth-world/

Common Misconceptions about Rape and Dating Violence

1. RAPE AND DATING VIOLENCE ONLY HAPPEN TO FEMALES

Although rape and dating violence are more commonly reported by females, this does not mean that males are unaffected. In fact, while the number of men reporting rape and dating violence is low, evidence suggests that the stigma of a male being raped or experiencing dating violence means his assault is less likely to be reported, as are fights or violence between males more generally. Even for males who do report rape or dating violence, there is concern that law enforcement or school officials may take their reports of abuse less seriously. There is also unnecessary and harmful stigma around males admitting they have been victimized, implying that they were "too weak" to fight off the perpetrator. In addition, there is the harmful perception that "men cannot be raped." These cultural myths lead to many male victims of rape or dating violence suffering alone and in silence. There is also the issue that some people believe that an erection proves that a man wants to have sex, but men have erections for all kinds of reasons, many of them unrelated to sexual activity. Between 90% and 95% of men who are raped fail to report it; furthermore, many men who have been raped categorize the experience as just another physical assault, perhaps to avoid questioning their sexual orientation. In addition, since ejaculation may occur during rape, many men hesitate to report their rapes because they fear that people will believe they enjoyed the experience or question their sexuality. For more information about dating violence and rape and who is at greatest risk of rape, see questions 2 and 9.

2. RAPISTS ARE USUALLY STRANGERS

The public perception is that rape is more likely between people who do not know one another, but the facts show that this is false. In fact, four out of five reported rapes happened between significant others, boyfriends, girlfriends, or spouses. Coerced sex, or consenting to sexual activity under pressure from a boyfriend or girlfriend, is also rape. Recent surveys show that 84% of female rape victims knew their attackers and that 57% of rapes occurred while on a date. Known as acquaintance rape, date rape, or hidden rape, this common occurrence only entered the public consciousness in the 1980s. On the other hand, only one in five rapes is perpetrated by a stranger, on average. When rape is perpetrated by someone the victim is familiar with, they are even less likely to report it than if it were a stranger. Some 90% of rape victims fail to report rape when committed by someone they know. While parents and teachers may warn us of the danger posed by strangers, the fact is that we face greater danger from people we know and trust. See questions 8 and 9 for more information about who typically rapes whom.

3. RAPE AND DATING VIOLENCE ONLY AFFECT HETEROSEXUAL COUPLES

While media attention focuses on rape and dating violence among heterosexual couples, people in gay and lesbian couples report at least as high a rate of rape and dating violence as heterosexual couples. Some 44% of lesbians and 61% of bisexual women report being raped or being a victim of domestic violence or stalking by an intimate partner. In addition, 26% of gay men and 37% of bisexual men report being raped or being a victim of domestic violence or stalking by an intimate partner. There are studies that suggest that the rates may be higher, but such reports are typically not taken as seriously by local law enforcement. In addition, the absence of gay and lesbian couples in media suggests that the sense of solidarity may prevent some gay or lesbian victims of rape and dating violence from reporting their assaults. As startling as these statistics may be, it is even worse for transgender people. One recent study found that nearly half of all transgender people report having been raped. While sexual orientation or gender identity does not cause rape, public perception among care providers may prevent victims from receiving the care they need and deserve. See questions 2, 9, 15, 39, and 41 for more information.

4. ROMEO AND JULIET LAWS ENSURE THAT CONSENSUAL SEX IS LEGAL, EVEN IF ONE PARTNER IS OVER THE AGE OF EIGHTEEN

Romeo and Juliet laws vary from state to state. These laws emerged as a reaction to statutory rape charges when two people close in age are in a consensual sexual relationship to prevent convictions for statutory rape. Some states have laws that exempt consensual sex between two minors or between a minor and an adult eighteen years or older if the relationship began prior to the older individual turning eighteen, while others consider any sexual activity with a minor rape or statutory rape. There are several ways that Romeo and Juliet laws help protect young people in consensual relationships: first, the charge may be reduced from a felony to a misdemeanor; second, there may be a reduction in charges; next, there may be an opportunity for the defendant to expunge their record; and finally, Romeo and Juliet laws may mean that the defendant does not have to register on the sex offender registry. See questions 4, 7, and 24 for more on this issue.

5. ALL A VICTIM OF DATING VIOLENCE NEEDS TO DO IS END THE ABUSIVE RELATIONSHIP

Ending the relationship with an abuser does not mean there are not repercussions. Many people who experience dating violence (or rape) may be traumatized for years afterward. Studies show that in the early days after an incident of rape or dating violence, up to 94 out of 100 women report symptoms of post-traumatic stress disorder (PTSD); nine months later, about 30 of the 100 women continued to report symptoms of PTSD. Symptoms of PTSD include fear, anxiety, stress, unusual nervousness, insomnia, difficulty concentrating, feeling hopeless or ashamed, and feelings of numbness or being out of it. If you have been raped or have experienced dating violence and find yourself experiencing one or more of these symptoms, it may be useful to find a counselor or therapist to speak to. Refer to questions 20, 21, 30, and 31 for more information.

QUESTIONS AND ANSWERS

❖

The Basics

1. What is dating violence?

Dating violence, also known as intimate partner violence or relationship abuse, can be defined as a pattern of behaviors that seek to exert power over the partner and control their behaviors. Dating violence can include physical violence or emotional, sexual, or verbal abuse. Whatever form it takes, this behavior is always about power and control. Moreover, dating violence can affect anyone in any relationship, male or female, nonbinary, polyamorous, straight, gay, lesbian, bisexual, or transgender. Dating violence can take many different forms, but there are some common themes. In terms of physical violence, the dominant partner may engage in punching, slapping, hairpulling, biting, shoving, choking, or burning the victim. Verbal or emotional violence includes undermining the victim's confidence or self-worth by swearing at, insulting, or belittling the person—often claiming it is "just a joke" when the victim protests that their feelings are hurt—or threatening to use a weapon, to confine the victim, or to harm the victim or their family members or a cherished pet.

In addition to physical violence and emotional or verbal abuse, significant others sometimes exert themselves on their partners sexually. Make no mistake, sexual violence between two people in a relationship is never okay, and it is never the victim's fault, even if the couple has had sex in the past. Sexual violence includes unwanted or inappropriate sexual touching, such as in public or in front of family members; pressure to consent to sexual activity; poking someone in the rear when they squat; attempted rape, rape, or attempting or having sex with a person who is intoxicated and unable to consent to sex; and sex with someone who is underage or unable to consent due to mental illness or another condition. All of these behaviors are about making the victim uncomfortable as they work to avoid these sorts of humiliating experiences.

In addition to these types of abuse, depending on the couple, digital violence or cyberstalking may occur. This happens when one person uses social media or technology to stalk or harass their partner by monitoring the person's activity; posting inappropriate things, including sexualized or otherwise vulnerable photos or videos; or demanding passwords to social media accounts. In addition, requiring access to a partner's cell phone and demands for contact lists are also forms of dating violence, as is exerting power and control of a partner's finances, prohibiting a partner from getting a job, or sabotaging a partner's job or job applications by not passing on messages from interested employers or actively bad-mouthing the partner to the potential employer. See question 12 on stalking and cyberstalking in this book. Furthermore, prohibiting a partner from maintaining friendships with friends or family members is also a form of dating violence. This is often done by claiming that the victim's family or friends do not really understand the victim or what they need—only the abuser does.

Regardless of what type of dating violence a person experiences, it is never the victim's fault. If you are a victim of dating violence, it is important to take it seriously as a problem in the relationship. Consider talking with a counselor, therapist, priest, or minister, either alone, with your partner, or with a trusted family member.

Unfortunately, dating violence is frequently a harbinger of future domestic violence if the relationship continues. Take this red flag seriously. Those who do not may experience more serious side effects of domestic violence, such as substance abuse, eating disorders, risky sexual behaviors, or experiencing domestic violence in later life. Treatment is essential to avoid some of these more serious consequences, and treatment is available in numerous venues; perhaps begin by browsing the resources section of this book and talking to a school counselor, nurse, minister, family friend, or trusted physician.

Historically speaking, dating violence was not a well-known phenomenon. For much of human history, people were frequently physically violent with one another, and there was little to no legal recourse or therapies to help victims, in particular cisgender, heterosexual women. People who were not cisgender or heterosexual had even less recognition or access to legal remedies or therapies. Rather, women who experienced dating violence tended to do one of two things: they shrugged it off as a bad date or their partner having a bad night and continued the relationship or they broke up with their dating partner. Regardless of the way dating violence was dealt with in the past, it certainly was not talked about extensively, and there were few, if any, resources available, especially for young people experiencing this type of violence.

With approximately one-third of all students in grades nine through twelve experiencing dating violence, this common occurrence can lead to a number of problems for victims, both now and later in life. Experiencing dating violence puts victims at higher risk of smoking (tobacco or otherwise), depression, anxiety, eating disorders, and having frequent sex with multiple partners, perhaps in an attempt to find the so-called right partner. Some victims may take the extreme measures of dating violence, such as constant vigilance over their whereabouts, as a sign of love—but it is not. It is controlling behavior that needs to stop to ensure the victim's safety. It poses a significant risk to the victim of the stalking behaviors, as there is no way to come out of the situation safely without intervention. It is of the utmost importance for victims to get the help they need to either end the relationship or to enter counseling, with their partner, if possible.

For women in particular and some men and nonbinary folks, a large part of their developmental identity is formed through their intimate relationships. Their relationships tell them about their self-worth and value in their communities. If that relationship is damaged or abusive, the female victim may experience a loss of self-esteem or perceived value. This is not to say that men are not affected, but men tend to form their developmental identity based on their independence from others; therefore, the impact may be somewhat less damaging.

Similarly, while there is little research on the long-term impacts of dating violence on the developing psyche, what has been found suggests that PTSD might be one of the developments that follows the experience. In addition, some victims may experience disassociation; they feel as if they are watching their lives from a third-person experience rather than firsthand. This dissociative state can feel as if the victim is watching their life as if it were a movie rather than happening in the present. This sort of out-of-body experience may be a sign that there is more to the dating violence than the victim wants to believe.

Typically, dating violence, in whatever form, has very little to do with sex or love, although that is the primary feature of the experience for the victim. For the person who commits dating violence, it is all about control, and it is frequently about ensuring that the victim stays true to the abuser. Dating violence is an early step toward gaining control over another person.

2. How common is dating violence in the United States and who is most likely to experience it?

Dating violence is probably a lot more common than you think. Nearly a third of adolescent youth report facing some sort of dating violence from their partners, and nearly 1.5 million high school students report physical abuse from a partner. Young women aged sixteen to twenty-four years old experience the highest rates of dating violence, nearly triple the national average, and their experience of dating violence or abusive behavior typically begins between ages twelve and eighteen. In addition, more than half of women and men aged eleven to twenty-four years old report experiencing physical or emotional abuse or violence. Ten percent of high school students report being hit, slapped, or kicked by an intimate partner. Unfortunately, those who have themselves been abused, whether as children by a parent or caregiver or in a dating relationship, are more likely to turn around and abuse others in their own future intimate relationships. Abuse that begins so early may lead to an increase in severity in abusive relationships in the future. In addition, LGBTQIA+ youth in particular are at an increased risk for dating or intimate partner violence, including sexual, physical, emotional, and verbal abuse.

However, high school is not the only place where people report dating violence. Some 43% of college women who are dating report experiencing violent and abusive dates, and 16% of college women report being sexually abused in a dating relationship. Physical violence is not the only type of abuse, though: 36% of college students who date report having given a partner their computer, online access to their email, or their social media passwords—all of which lead to a greater risk of digital dating abuse, including uploading of unflattering or embarrassing photos or videos, awkward or inappropriate status updates, and other sorts of cringeworthy unwanted postings. This sort of behavior can best be described as cyberbullying or cyberstalking. Adding to this problem is the fact that 67% of victims do not report their experience of dating violence to anyone, much less law enforcement officials, perhaps because they do not think of digital dating abuse as a problem, or they are embarrassed to be in an abusive relationship, or they fear what others will say or think about them or their partner if they do come forward. In addition, emotional and verbal abuse, while less physical, can be just as impactful on the victim's life. While parents and others might want to help and typically believe that they can spot the signs of dating violence, in a survey, only 58% of parents could identify all the signs of dating violence. For more information, see the signs of dating violence in the resources section of this book.

Given the data on dating violence, it is likely that you or someone you know has experienced dating violence. If a friend is experiencing dating violence, it can be an important first step to invite them to talk about it with you. Do not be surprised if they deny that what they are experiencing is abuse, at least at first. If you are experiencing dating violence, it is crucial that you speak about your experience with someone you trust. Everyone should know that dating violence can take many forms and that it typically increases in severity over time rather than diminishing. It is vital that a person experiencing dating violence escape the relationship before things get much worse. The truth is that the most dangerous time in a physically violent relationship—whether dating or domestic—is when the abused person seeks help; this seems to serve as a catalyst for even worse behavior, as the abuser realizes that they are about to lose control over the person they thought they owned or were able to control (at least emotionally).

As with domestic violence when we are older, dating violence tends to get worse over time, and in many ways, dating violence should be seen as a precursor for future domestic violence. In fact, without intervention, teen dating violence can lead to homicide of the partner or victim or of the parents or other relatives of the victim's family. While the statistics show a small pool of victims who are murdered, that number is not zero, so special care must be taken to extricate oneself from this sort of intimate partner violence. These situations become even more dire when a firearm is involved, accounting for some 61% of cases involving dating violence and homicide. Yet other cases involved victims who were pregnant and the abuser either did not want the baby or feared being charged with statutory rape because of his partner's age.

Part of the problem with dating violence stems from a lack of understanding of physical boundaries in intimate partner relationships. Young women and men engage in acts that others might consider violent, as if they are merely horseplay, but in fact, they set the stage for larger problems. As partners become more familiar with their bodies through intimacy, there is a temptation to play with the other in a somewhat aggressive manner. The lack of experience in intimate partnerships means that both partners, regardless of sexual orientation, are learning about these relationships for the first time and have likely had little guidance on what constitutes a good or bad relationship. The media does not help this at all; it glamorizes the dating or sexual violence that frequently shows up in pulp fiction, films, and music videos. In addition, no relationship is 100% good or bad; like most things involving humans, there is a mix of the good and the bad in our early intimate partner relationships as we all learn what we like and do not like in a partner.

One of the biggest differences between teen dating violence and adult domestic violence is the question of independence. In most cases, teens in intimate partnerships do not depend on their partner for food, clothing, and shelter, although some do live with their significant other's parents while finishing school, which makes them extra vulnerable. Others may depend on their partner for emotional validation, a sense of security in an uncertain world, or social security within a group of friends. Some look to their partner for the security and comfort that they cannot find at home, for whatever reason. Breaking up with an abuser is never easy and will most likely lead to a sense of loss on the part of the victim and rage on the part of the abuser.

3. What are the signs of dating violence?

The signs of dating violence may appear before a relationship is estab-lished. In fact, it is during the early stages that many red flags are revealed. For example, some relationships start with what might be termed a charm offensive or a too-good-to-be-true courtship. That too-good-to-be-true phase should be a red flag for everyone surrounding the target of this behavior. In this phase, the target (or future victim) may be swept off their feet—nearly every romantic gesture imaginable may be used. Per-haps the potential significant other shows up unexpectedly at your work because they were "thinking of you," perhaps the person sends numerous text messages asking you for a date; or perhaps the person tells all of your friends how much they care about you. These gestures are designed to break down the target's boundaries, whether the abuser realizes it or not. It is vitally important that the target establishes and maintains boundaries with people who want their time and attention, as it is the only way to prevent this sort of behavior.

Once boundaries have been breached, it is easy for the abuser to demand to know your location; limit your access to friends or family; crit-icize you or things and people you love; attempt to control how you look, what you wear, or how you earn or spend your own money; mock those things that bring you pleasure (e.g., movies, TV shows, music); or touch you in public in ways that make you uncomfortable. While these warning signs are seemingly innocuous, others are yet more invasive. One of the ways that an abuser controls the target is through humiliation, frequently in public, so that the victim is embarrassed and will do anything to avoid that sort of experience again. Closely related to public humiliation, verbal insults are designed to further denigrate the victim, whether the abuser intends them to or not. These include talking about a feature or habit of the victim that the abuser makes fun of or other things that are not choices, although those are open for critique too.

Physical violence is designed to keep the victim in a state of terror, consciously or subconsciously on the part of the abuser. There is frequently a period of heightened attention to the abuser as the victim works to avoid a blowup. Inevitably, these attempts fail, and the abuser blows up into a rage over something seemingly trivial. All of these, along with unpredictable mood swings, serve to control the behavior of the victim. The more the victim feels as if they are walking on eggshells around the abuser, the greater control the abuser is able to exert. In fact, paradoxically, abusers frequently think of themselves as the victims in the relationship and will blame their partners for "causing" the abuse. Some of this language includes, "If you didn't make me mad, I wouldn't X" or "If you had done X on time, I wouldn't have these outbursts." As with other sorts of victim blaming, this is done to avoid recognizing their own participation in the power dynamic between them and their partner and to avoid accountability for their own emotions and the consequences of their actions. This cycle is akin to the cycle of domestic violence, in that there is a honeymoon period, then a period of increasing tension, then a blowup, and then a reconciliation with a promise that it will never happen again. Unfortunately, those promises are about as permanent as the honeymoon period itself. To learn more about the cycle of abuse, see question 15 in this book.

The abuser may demand physical or sexual activity that you might not be ready to participate in, using phrases such as, "If you loved me, you would do X" or "My ex did this; if you want to keep me, you'll do it too." This behavior is not limited to teens or young adults; dating violence occurs at all ages and happens regardless of sexual orientation. But the problem is particularly acute in teens and young adults. They are typically learning how healthy relationships work for the first time, and if that first time is with an abuser, it can set the victim up for future dating or domestic violence, as that disturbing familiarity sometimes causes us to be attracted to people we otherwise would not be.

In addition, dating violence also affects the LGBTQIA+ community, where verbal abuse and pressure to engage in sexual activity takes an even darker turn when targets are required to "prove" their sexual orientation by performing certain sexual acts upon command by their abuser. This is frequently accompanied by attempts to shame the victim into doing sexual or other acts that the victim does not want to do—as if not doing the act means that the abuser will tell everyone that the victim is a phony. Sometimes they are acts that the victim might want to participate in later on, after becoming comfortable with their partner. However, the partner's insistence on doing the acts at a certain time ensures that sexual activity in the future will sometimes reflect that past trauma and can make future intimate connections more challenging.

Despite embarrassment being a common feature for victims experiencing abuse, it is important to get help nonetheless. The victim tends to buy into the abuser's story that it is all the victim's fault. If you think you are in a relationship that has become violent or one in which your boundaries are ignored, it is critical that you seek help using resources from the resources section of this book or from a counselor, therapist, or other resource, including dialing 911 if you feel as if you are in immediate danger.

4. What is consent and why does it matter?

There are several components to consent—and it is more than merely saying yes to any sort of sexual activity one time. Consent includes what you feel comfortable doing with your partner and excludes things you are not comfortable with; these activities will likely change over time, but the common theme is that you are comfortable doing whatever sexual activity you are about to be engaged in. Essentially, consent is largely about respecting people's boundaries and learning about one another, both emotionally and sexually. Learning how to ask for consent is a crucial part of a person's work toward having healthy sexual relationships (and boundaries) with other people.

For consent to be valid, the person agreeing to sexual activity must be cognizant, conscious, and aware of what they are agreeing to; this is known as having the capacity for consent. This means that people who are inebriated, high, or otherwise impaired are unable to give consent; this is known as not having the capacity to consent. In addition, people with limited mental capacity or learning disabilities frequently cannot provide consent; indeed, their capacity for consent is questionable and is most frequently seen as similar to children being unable to consent to sexual activity. Consent in these cases means that the person must know the physical acts they are agreeing to, the psychological and emotional impact of those acts, and the physical consequences of the act (e.g., sexually transmitted diseases, unintended pregnancy). For more information on young adults consenting to sexual activity with someone older than eighteen years old, see question 24 in this book on so-called Romeo and Juliet laws.

Furthermore, consent can be withdrawn at any time, even after sexual activity has begun and even if the participants have participated in sexual activity in the past. This also means that consenting to one activity does not mean that other activities are implicitly agreed to. Essentially, consent is an agreement between two people that sexual activity is something both of them want to have happen right then, and it is very specific to that particular sexual encounter and that specific sexual activity. Consent should be reaffirmed throughout the act; do not automatically assume your partner still wants to have sex just because they consented to kissing, cuddling, or touching.

In addition, couples that have been together for some time may feel that their partner knows what they want and that they do not have to ask for consent. Consent is not a onetime deal for long-term relationships either: consent must be affirmed each time a couple decides to engage in sexual activity, and either partner has an equal right to say no to sex, regardless of age, sexual orientation, history of sexual activity, or any other considerations. While our culture used to condone sexual activity without consent between married partners, reflecting the prevailing opinion at the time that marriage meant that a woman gave consent to all future sexual activity and was, in effect, her husband's property, it has been against the law across the United States since 1993.

Consent matters because it is part of building healthy relationships. If you want to have a long-lasting, mutually nurturing relationship that includes sexual activity, then consent is an important component of mutually satisfying sexual activity; in fact, it can be made a fun part of foreplay. If a person does not consent or is unable to consent, that means that the sexual activity is actually sexual assault or rape; the person having nonconsensual sex is committing sexual assault or rape and in extreme circumstances may find themselves arrested and prosecuted. There literally is no such thing as nonconsensual sex; it is rape or sexual assault in every instance. In addition, a person who is pressured to engage in sexual activity cannot consent to the act, given that coercion, or forceful persuasion, negates the consent: that is, pressuring someone to have sex with you means that you have sexually assaulted or raped your partner if sexual activity happens afterward.

Think of consent as a contract: both parties agree to one or more activities, but either party may withdraw their consent at any time. Since nobody wants to deal with the legal or emotional aftermath of sexual assault or rape, it is best to ensure that your partner is an eager and willing participant in every part of your sexual encounter every time you have sex with them. If you or a friend find yourselves accused of rape or sexual assault, serious consideration needs to be given that you (or they) may have crossed a line that should have been avoided.

5. How should consent be asked for and given?

Consent can begin well before sexual activity is considered and should be part of every step in a relationship. Begin by asking easier, nonsexual questions, such as asking your future partner out for coffee or to a movie and asking whether they would like that. Perhaps build your relationship on a shared interest in pleasing one another. This can help to set the mood of respecting one another's mutual boundaries. We can see examples of asking for consent in old movies, where a person asks another, "May I kiss you?" or "Would you mind if I kiss you?" It is far less embarrassing to ask for consent for a kiss and be turned down than to misread the signals and go in for it anyway and find yourself rejected or kissing someone's ear. Nobody wants that kind of awkwardness with a new love interest.

Asking for consent to sexual activity, when asked for in a pleasing way, can help build the mood rather than killing it. Asking for consent throughout the sexual encounter can ensure that you and your partner are both happy with the activities you do together. In fact, consent can be part of sexual foreplay, as you and your partner ask increasingly sexual questions. It can be as simple as, "May I X?" or "I'd like to X" or "Would you like for me to X?" As long as your partner agrees to each and every act you two do together, you are in good shape as far as consent goes and can avoid a lot of the trouble that can occur if you had not asked in the first place. It may also lead to conversations about what your partner prefers; if you ask your partner if you may do one thing, they may suggest another activity or place on their body they would like to be touched or they may suggest a different type of touch.

It is important to bear in mind that consent to one activity does not imply consent to anything else. If your partner is uncomfortable with anything you would like to do, you must back off or risk crossing a line that most of us want to avoid. Asking for consent in a manner that shows you respect your partner may allow them to say yes to activities that they might not otherwise think they would enjoy. That means that you have more choices in terms of sexual activities than if you had never asked for consent in the first place. Think of consent as your road map to pleasure with your partner: every turn or move leads you both closer to your destination.

When your partner asks for your consent to an activity, take a moment to think about it. Do not say yes just because you really like them or want them to like or love you or because you think everyone else you know is doing it. Instead, say yes if you really want to do (or have done to you) the things your partner has asked for you to consent to. If you are not comfortable with an activity, say so to your partner but perhaps also offer an alternative activity or postpone that particular activity to a future date when you think you might feel more comfortable. Refusing a particular act should not be seen as a sign that the relationship is over or doomed: rather, it is a sign that the relationship is healthy and that both partners respect one another and each other's boundaries.

The most important thing about consent is learning how to ask for it and how to give it. This is one of the most important parts of intimate relationships and often does not receive the attention it deserves. Instead of it always being one partner's job, try alternating who asks for which activity. Perhaps make it a game during foreplay or incorporate the language of consent to everyday activities: "Would you like to X?" or "May I X?" Although it might sound old-fashioned, respecting one another's boundaries will help ensure a more mutually satisfying experience for both partners and that there are no misunderstandings about boundaries.

6. What is rape?

Simply put, rape is sexual activity without consent. If consent is cognizant and conscious and involves an awareness of what is being agreed to, then rape is sexual activity when the partner cannot or does not agree to sexual activity, or is underage, or suffers from a mental illness or learning disability that prevents their consenting to sexual activity. That means that a partner who is drunk, high, unconscious, or otherwise impaired cannot give consent and should be taken care of rather than forced to have sex that they cannot fully appreciate or participate in. Rape involves penetration—oral, vaginal, or anal—with a penis, other body part, or a foreign object. Rape is typically not about passion or desire for the other person; rather, it is an expression of power over someone who cannot prevent sexual activity from happening.

In the distant past, legally, rape was a property crime, as women were considered the property of the male head of household, and some of these ideas remain in our culture. In the earliest legal codes, rape was not considered problematic except for women without a male head of household, such as a widow. For most women in Anglo-Saxon England, their rapist could be forgiven his rape if he paid what was known as *wergild*, which was graduated depending on the social class of the victim and her father or other head of household; this payment system ensured that clans avoided blood feuds for something as minor (at the time) as raping a woman. As laws evolved, numerous wrinkles in the legal system evolved too. For example, unless a woman was bruised or injured or she had screamed for help or otherwise brought attention to her sexual assault, she was largely not believed.

During the Norman invasion of England in 1066, William the Conqueror declared that any man who raped an Anglo-Saxon woman was to be publicly blinded and castrated, the thinking being that these were the body parts that had caused his transgression; this public punishment ensured that rape was quite infrequent during the invasion. After the Norman invasion, much like today, many cases of rape were ignored or the assailant let off with a slap on the wrist. During the fourteenth century, some heiresses were abducted and raped; a so-called solution to this problem was for these women to be forced to marry their rapists, a particularly attractive route to success for men with few scruples and fewer financial prospects. This sort of "solution" still exists in parts of the world where women are seen as objects rather than people with their own dreams and desires. In the early modern period in England, most cases that made their way into the court system were rapes of women of higher social status or children who turned up with sexually transmitted diseases.

Many of the excuses used by rapists nowadays have their origin in these early attitudes: either the woman had had sex with the man in the past, and therefore it could not be rape; the woman had sex with other men, and therefore it could not be rape; or the rape happened when the man was out of town—this excuse was aided by the fact that until the refinement of the microscope by Leeuwenhoek (around 1673), people had no idea how conception actually worked. There were numerous erroneous thoughts about reproduction, including that a normal pregnancy could last anywhere from five to fourteen months, depending on the so-called perfection of the child (i.e., male); of course, we know that is not true and that most pregnancies last forty weeks, or about nine months. In addition to this problematic thought, people of the early modern period also believed that female orgasm was required for conception to occur; this led to the false belief that conception proved consent—a particularly convenient ideology for men of the time. The age of consent was established in England in 1576 at the age of ten years old, which for many of us seems far too young. The medical system reinforced the legal system, which, in turn, reinforced the medical system. These ideologies worked hand in glove to ensure that most women who were raped remained silent. Indeed, in the past, speaking about your rape was a guarantee that you were unchaste, or lacked sexual propriety, as speaking about sexual matters was seen as disqualifying a woman from that virtue.

Rape is also frequently used as a tactic against an enemy during wartime. The thinking goes that women who are raped by the enemy may be rejected by their husbands or partners, as they have been defiled by the enemy, and the child that they might produce will be 50% the genetic product of the enemy, thus leading to a weakening of the bloodlines of their enemies. Rape is also used as a means of revenge against an enemy during wartime; during wars, men from most every country have been reported as having raped local women, and this was seen as a near inevitable consequence of wartime activity. Nowadays, rape is considered a criminal act under international rules of war, and most rapists face military jail time or the death penalty for their crimes.

7. What is statutory rape?

Statutory rape is any sexual activity with a minor, but the age at which it is deemed statutory rape as opposed to consensual sexual activity differs from state to state in the United States. Every state has its own laws on what constitutes statutory rape, but there are some commonalities. First, every state prohibits sexual activity with anyone who is twelve years old or younger, especially if the perpetrator is two or more years older than the victim. If, however, force is involved, the perpetrator may instead be charged with child molestation or rape, and the consequences are likewise much more serious and likely will include jail time as well as a lifetime requirement to be on the sex offender registry.

Statutory rape is different from other rape cases in that it is about the age of the younger of the two participants and whether they are legally able to consent to sexual activity. Although the legal system used to treat adult females engaging in sexual activity with younger men more lightly than adult men with younger women, this is no longer the case. Previously, adult women having sex with much younger men was frequently seen as desirable rather than as an assault, as can be seen in numerous media representations in movies, music videos, and other media. Since that time, thankfully, much has changed. In fact, women who sexually assault or engage in sexual activity with much younger men are frequently given much harsher prison sentences than men convicted of the same crime, as if their crimes were any different or as if women who do these things are somehow worse than the men who also commit statutory rape. Generally speaking, this has to do with the gendered notion that women should all be nurturers, despite all the evidence to the contrary. In addition, two minors engaged in sexual activity with one another may find themselves charged with the statutory rape of their partner, regardless of their partner's willingness to engage in sexual activity. In addition to fines, many people found guilty of statutory rape also serve some time in prison and must register as a sex offender for the rest of their lives.

Another group for whom sexual activity cannot be agreed to is people with developmental delays, or learning disabilities, as they are considered to not be able to consent to the physical, emotional, and other changes that may occur if they were to engage in sexual activity, regardless of their age.

The penalties for statutory rape are considerable. Punishment may include a fine, significant jail time, and being placed on the sex offender registry, which can have lifetime repercussions. Part of consideration in cases of statutory rape is whether the minor or mentally incapacitated person consented to sexual activity or if force was involved. In many cases, the person convicted of statutory rape must register as a sex offender for the rest of their lives, thus limiting many of their future opportunities, including those related to employment or housing.

The punishment for those who engaged in sexual activity with a minor who lied about their age is somewhat of a gray area in the legal system. There have been cases where an accused person successfully defended themselves against statutory rape charges given that they reasonably believed the minor was an adult at the time of their sexual encounter. Part of the evidence in these cases might include fake identification that shows an age older than the minor actually is or behavior by the minor that suggested they were older than they are. This is only part of the reason that a fake ID is such a bad idea—it gives other people an idea about us that puts us in danger.

Additionally, in some areas, there may be different ages of consent for same-sex encounters as opposed to heterosexual sexual encounters. More conservative states tend to treat homosexual interactions more harshly, while more liberal states take a more enlightened approach. If in doubt, check your local law for guidance. See the directory of resources in this text for links to websites that can show you how to do this.

8. What is the difference between rape, sexual assault, and sexual abuse?

Rape and sexual assault share many features, including the lack of consent to sexual activity. In addition, both of these are crimes with severe punishments. However, rape includes unwanted penetration, whether vaginal, oral, or anal, with a penis, other body part, or other object. Rape can happen when a person is intoxicated or otherwise unable to consent to sexual activity, whether due to substance use or abuse, mental impairment, or age at the time of sexual activity. Contrary to popular belief and frequent messaging from the media, parents, and others, the threat of rape or sexual assault is not primarily from strangers. While most of us were warned about "stranger danger," the fact is that most rapes happen between people who already know one another. People who rape can be neighbors, former neighbors, teachers, coaches, mentors, family members, intimate partners, or former intimate partners. The danger of rape by a random stranger is less than the media might suggest. One study found that rapists attacked total strangers fewer than 25% of the time.

Sexual assault includes unwanted touching, kissing, groping, or other inappropriate contact that is unwanted, frequently in the absence of a request for consent. It also includes things such as molestation, catcalling or whistling at someone, exposure of the genitals to another person, surreptitious viewing of other people while they are naked, and the sharing of explicit photos without the consent of the person in the photographs; this means things such as revenge porn are definitely a type of sexual assault. Similar to the statistics regarding rape, sexual assault victims most frequently tend to know their assailant prior to being sexually assaulted.

Sexual assault and sexual abuse sound similar and share some similarities, in that the touching or interacting with someone is unwanted, but that is where the similarities end. Sexual abuse involves unwanted touching, kissing, groping, or other inappropriate contact that is unwanted, but the victim is typically much younger than the perpetrator, most frequently children or other young people. The age of consent varies across the country but ranges from sixteen to eighteen years of age, and any sexual activity, wanted or unwanted, younger than these ages equals sexual abuse and perhaps sexual assault if the person having sex with the teenager is over the age of eighteen. Regardless of age, it is important to bear in mind that unwanted sexual activity or pressuring someone to have sexual activity is entirely inappropriate, can be a criminal act that will be prosecuted by the local authorities, and may lead to a lengthy prison sentence, fines, and potentially a requirement to register on the sex offender list for the rest of perpetrator's life.

If you find that you have unexplainable bruising, tenderness, difficulty walking, or other injuries, potentially including broken bones, after a night of intoxication or illicit drug use, it may be that you were raped while you were inebriated or otherwise impaired. Before cleaning yourself, showering, or changing clothes, consider going to a hospital and telling them about your experience. If you choose to do this, know that it may be useful to have a trusted friend with you, someone who might be able to fill in some of the gaps in your memory from being intoxicated or impaired. If you are under the age of consent in your state and you experience these unexplained injuries after a night of drinking, consider going to your family doctor or a local clinic, as you may have been sexually abused, assaulted, or raped. In fact, people who abuse young adults frequently use access to alcohol or drugs as a means of building trust with the young person and reducing that person's inhibitions. You should know that your medical provider will be unable to tell your family about your assault without your express permission.

9. How common is rape in the United States and who is most likely to become a victim of rape or sexual assault?

Both men and women, cisgender and trans, and young and old are at risk for rape, although that risk differs based on gender identity, sexual orientation, and other factors, most of which are out of our control. On average, there are over 300,000 rape victims over the age of twelve every year. That means that a rape occurs roughly every minute and a half. The majority of these people are young, between eighteen and thirty-four years old. Under the age of eighteen, law enforcement in most states consider rape to be child sexual abuse, and it is treated differently than rape of an adult, someone past the age of consent, or someone over the age of eighteen. In addition, many states regulate who may have consensual sex with someone who is at least sixteen years old, with most finding that a two-year age difference is acceptable (see question 24 in this text for more information on Romeo and Juliet laws). A person who has sex with a minor who is two or more years younger can be charged with statutory rape, although these laws vary greatly from state to state.

Justice Department publications reveal that 68% of all rapes are *never* reported to authorities. That means that only about 32% of rapes *are* reported, and out of that number, even fewer reach the court system. Part of the problem is that some victims wait to report their assault and lose evidence by cleaning themselves afterward. In addition, another Justice Department report finds that 35% of sexual assault victims are unclear whether what happened to them was a crime or if there was harm intended by their attacker. These questions can cause someone who was raped to not report their experience to authorities, as they try to simply move past their trauma.

One out of every six women reports being raped or having rape attempted upon her, while one out of thirty-three men report being raped or having rape attempted upon him. This means most women know someone who has been raped or have had rape attempted upon them, while most men do not. Most alarmingly, one in seven rape victims is a child under the age of six years old. While men typically face less risk of rape, young men are at particular risk, with men ages sixteen to twenty-four four times more likely of experiencing rape than the average population, and college-aged males, eighteen to twenty-four years old, are three times more likely to experience rape. Among college-aged females, Black women have the highest risk, at 68%, compared to their white peers, at 57%. Hispanic women seem to be at a somewhat lower risk in comparison to their white counterparts, 8% and 20%, respectively, of lifetime sexual assault or rape. There is some evidence that prior victimization, either molestation or sexual abuse as a young person, increases the risk of sexual assault or rape among college-aged females.

On the other hand, Native American youth are twice the risk of sexual assault or rape in comparison to their non-Native peers. In addition, people in prisons more frequently experience sexual assault or rape, and these institutions lack sufficient protocols for reporting these acts or for prosecuting the perpetrators of these attacks. It appears that people in prisons are likely to face sexual assault or rape from both other inmates and the guards who are allegedly there to protect them; while men appear to be equally victimized by inmates or guards, it appears that women inmates are at even greater risk of abuse from prison guards.

Some 83% of disabled females and 32% of disabled males are victims of sexual violence. In addition, the elderly are another vulnerable population, with elderly women at the greatest risk of sexual assault or rape. Only some 30% of all these victims report their assault to the authorities.

Of those that are reported, even fewer find their way into a court case against the rapist for a variety of reasons, including police officers not taking the claim seriously (i.e., not following up with the victim or the perpetrator, not taking witness statements), not collecting evidence or providing testing in a timely manner, or having a district attorney who is unwilling to bring the perpetrator to court to preserve their conviction record. Given that most district attorneys are elected to that position, their conviction rate is seen as a barometer of their ability to do the job; bring too many rape cases that are not won, the thinking goes, and you find yourself back to practicing law on your own.

People enlisted in the military are also at an increased risk for rape or sexual assault, with some 25% of women reporting sexual assault and 80% of women reporting being harassed. In addition, male military members are also at an increased risk of sexual assault or rape compared to their nonmilitary peers, with some 7,500 men reporting assaults in 2019. There are several factors that make sexual assault or rape among military members more prevalent: first, there is the hypermasculine ideology of dominance, self-sufficiency, and risk-taking; next, there is the patriarchal structure of the military, with members expected to resolve their differences with their peers themselves rather than through the formalized chain of command; and finally, the military's culture of homophobia may lead some homophobic and sexually insecure members to assault men they perceive as weaker or less masculine than they are as a paradoxical demonstration of their heterosexuality. As with other rapes, the presence of alcohol or illicit drugs increases the risk of these troubling behaviors.

The numbers of reported sexual assaults and rapes among military members are increasing, likely due to a change in climate that encourages reporting these assaults; however, reporting from male military personnel lags significantly behind their female counterparts. It should be said that reporting sexual assault or rape while in the military is not without its dangers; harassment or retaliation frequently happens to those who report their assault or rape, leading many victims to end their relationship with the military or for their attackers to seek vengeance against them, victimizing their prey once again and causing emotional, psychological, or physical damage, up to and including murder.

For everyone outside the military, the risks significantly increase for folks in the LGBTQIA+ community, with trans folks experiencing an elevated risk of rape or sexual assault when compared to their cisgender peers. Some 44% of lesbians and 61% of bisexual women experience rape, physical violence, or stalking by an intimate partner, compared to 35% of heterosexual women, or nearly double the rate of victimization.

Meanwhile, 26% of gay men and 37% of bisexual men experience rape, physical violence, or stalking, compared to 29% of straight men reporting similar experiences. For trans folks, the numbers are even more dire: 47% of transgender people report being sexually assaulted during their lifetime.

10. What are the signs of rape?

Some physical signs of rape include bruising, vaginal or anal bleeding, difficulty walking, soreness, and broken or dislocated bones. There are more subtle emotional signs that a victim may have been raped, including PTSD, flashbacks, nightmares, anxiety, or depression. There may be periods of intense sadness, loss of energy or interest in activities previously enjoyed, feeling hopeless, outbursts of unexplained crying, suicidal thoughts, dissociation or a feeling that you are out of your body, or being unable to focus on work or school. Rape can also leave victims less trusting of people, for good reason. Or they may be worried and anxious about meeting new people, angry and shocked, or uncontrollably shaky—as in trembling for no apparent reason. They may also experience shortness of breath or chronic fatigue syndrome. Other side effects can include self-blame, a tendency to self-medicate with alcohol or illicit drugs, sexual promiscuity, feelings of worthlessness, or a feeling that they did something to deserve their victimization.

In addition, young people who have been raped tend to find themselves thinking negatively about themselves, and this can sometimes lead to dropping out of school; if this happens, there can be a lifelong impact on the victim's earning ability or their ability to take care of themselves and the ones they care about in the future. While most young people are not so concerned about their lifetime earning potential, most of us would like to live comfortably, and dropping out of high school decreases the chances of that happening. If you do drop out of high school, you should know that the general equivalency diploma (GED) scores sometimes work as college admissions testing too, so be sure to get your GED as soon as possible after quitting high school—it makes the test easier (although not easy).

In addition, victims may engage in risky sexual behavior (in addition to promiscuity); suffer from insomnia; adopt risky lifestyle habits, such as drinking excessively, using drugs, or smoking; engage in self-mutilation; have issues trusting intimate partners again; experience parenting stress if they already have children, making children act as parents to tend to their parent's pain; or suffer early or premature births or postpartum depression.

These harms are intensified if a rape victim is coerced into carrying a fetus to term that began as a result of rape.

For many victims, it is hard to determine whether their experience was rape. There may be confusion about how and when things happened, and inebriation or other drug use can cloud one's memory. One factor that leads to underreporting of rape crimes is the warning that we all grew up with about "stranger danger." Most of us were taught to avoid dark alleys because some bad person might assault us there. The simple truth is that people we already know or love are the ones most likely to rape us, including friends and classmates or an instructor, coach, family member, community member, boss, minister or priest, or other individual. This contributes to the problem of knowing whether an experience was rape, because if it was, then our acquaintance is a rapist—something many victims are reluctant to acknowledge because of their pervious relationship with their rapist. For some people, it can be difficult to acknowledge that this person they have thought so highly of for some time could do such a thing to them.

Another factor in the confusion over whether what one has experienced was rape or not is the problem our parents all warn us about: hanging with the wrong crowd. Sometimes the wrong crowd is a problem, to be sure, but the kids that our parents do not worry so much about us being with, whether it is in scouting, a youth group at church, extracurricular sports or academic clubs, or any otherwise wholesome activities, can also become a threat to us.

Regardless of what you wore, what you said or did not say, or whether you had sex with the perpetrator in the past, if you did not want to have sex with that person at that time, it is not your fault. Sometimes people who are being sexually assaulted find that they are frozen—as if they are incapable of moving, screaming, or fighting off the assault. If that happens, it does not mean that you were not assaulted; rather, it means that you had one of the three responses to threat: fight, flight, or freeze. Given that our culture acknowledges only two threat responses, many victims have a hard time justifying their inaction. In addition, sometimes people who are raped or sexually assaulted may find that their body's response did not match their mental state, as sometimes the body climaxes due to stimulus regardless of the person's unwillingness to participate in sexual activity; this can lead to even more confusion about the encounter, as the victim is unsure of whether they wanted the sexual activity or not. For some victims who experience climax, the juxtaposition of saying no and their body's apparently positive response make it difficult to determine whether the experience was rape or whether others will believe them when they tell them they were raped.

If you think that what you experienced might have been rape, it is important to seek professional medical help immediately, before you shower, sleep, or do anything else. This does not mean you are required to report the incident as rape to the police, but you may want to protect your right to do so if you decide that you need to do that. If it is too late for that, then you should be sure to speak to a trusted counselor, physician, or teacher so that they can help you find the counseling or other therapeutic methods to help you fully heal from the assault.

11. How common are rape and dating violence around the world?

Unfortunately, rape and dating violence are common around the world. Nearly a billion women and girls around the world will experience rape or dating violence during their lifetime. Typically, laws worldwide do little to prevent or punish rape or dating violence, and in some cases, counterintuitively, the law encourages victims to remain silent after their experience rather than seeking justice for themselves. These laws either focus on "solving" the so-called problem, oftentimes by allowing the rapist to marry the victim; or allow rape between married couples; or require outside evidence of an attempted rape, including witnesses; or allow the rapist to impugn the dignity or reputation of the victim, thus leading to a reduction in prosecution and potential sentencing, if sentencing happens at all.

The United Nations International Children's Emergency Fund (UNICEF) has found that one out of every ten girls, some 120 million worldwide, has experienced forced intercourse or other sexual acts. Although governments around the world have indicated their desire to prohibit and punish rape and dating violence, few have been effective in causing a reduction in rapes and dating violence. In fact, if there was an international focus on eliminating rape and dating violence, there is little doubt that the rate of assaults would decline. In February 2017, the United Nations Women's Center found that rape is largely ignored as a global epidemic. Rape of a woman or girl by her husband is legal in ten out of eighty-two jurisdictions (countries); a solution to rape in nine jurisdictions (out of the eighty-two surveyed) is for the rapist to marry his victim; a financial settlement can eliminate charges of rape in at least twelve jurisdictions; the penalties for paid sex with a minor are frequently lower than those of other forms of rape of a minor; and rape is treated as a moral outrage and questions of the victim's honor or chastity are accepted elements of the legal system in fifteen jurisdictions. There are also places where a medical examiner must confirm the physical signs of rape, but in many cases, there are far too few of these medical examiners or they are located in population centers and inaccessible to women in rural areas. Judicial discretion allows judges to determine what material to allow into evidence or when to reduce charges.

Rape can be seen as the extreme outcome of sexual harassment, where perpetrators care less about their victim's interest or consent and more about expressing their own power over the victim. If seen this way, it becomes apparent why child sexual abuse, incest, and rapes of people who are too young to consent are so prevalent. Street harassment of women is designed to curtail women's sense of freedom in the public sphere and frequently for men to express their power over women in front of their peers. In many cultures, especially ones where there is a culture of machismo, men own the public spaces, and their dominance there is maintained by their demonstrations of power over the women who are unfortunate enough to catch their attention. This also leads to some of these same men restricting access to public spaces for their own female family members because of how dangerous it is out there, a danger that they themselves create and participate in.

A survey of women in India in 2016, found that 44% of women admitted to having been groped in public. Neighboring Bangladesh fared much worse, with 84% of women reporting having experienced derogatory comments or sexual advances in public. In Egypt, 99% of women across seven different regions have experienced sexual harassment, while some 37% of Arab women report experiencing sexual violence at some time in their lives. Some 50% of women in Tanzania report experiencing violence at the hands of their spouses or partners, and 43% of girls in Nigeria are married before the age of eighteen. In South Africa, 80% of surveyed women report having experienced some form of abuse within the last year. There are numerous reasons for these numbers in Africa and the Middle East: in addition to child marriages, some countries practice female genital mutilation—a practice steeped in the tradition of female chastity prior to marriage—and others have laws that let rapists go free while all the shame of the attack falls on the victim. All too frequently, a woman's rape is seen as shameful for her and her family, and this can lead to what is known as an honor killing, where a family murders their own family member for having been victimized.

Meanwhile, in the Americas, 65% of U.S. women surveyed report having experienced street harassment, 23% have been sexually harassed, and 37% express feeling unsafe when out alone at night. Rape in North America typically occurs within the home and is typically perpetrated by someone the victim already knows. Latin American women face many of the same problems as those found in Asia, as harassment is frequently laughed off as a nonserious issue. Some 86% of Brazilian women report having experienced harassment or violence in public places; what is more shocking is that 84% of Brazilian women report having been sexually harassed by the police. Furthermore, 96% of women in Mexico City report experiencing sexual violence in public spaces, and 58% report having been groped in public. Part of the reason for this behavior is believed to be that it is a society where men feel a sense of entitlement, where there is little public awareness that this is an actual problem, and where there is an overcrowded transit system and women working late or odd hours.

In Europe, the rate of experiencing physical and sexual violence ranges from a low of 35% in Germany to a high of 52% in Denmark. When the data is analyzed, it is found that European women are more likely to experience physical and sexual violence if their partner is from Latvia, Scandinavia, or Great Britain. In Great Britain, 64% of women report having experienced sexual harassment in public places.

Women in Australia have fared no better. In fact, 87% of Australian women report experiencing verbal or physical street harassment, and 40% report feeling unsafe when walking in their own neighborhoods at night. Some 77% of women in Papua New Guinea report experiencing sexual violence on public transportation, and non-intimate partner, or stranger, rape in public places is unfortunately a regular occurrence. Some of the reasons for this include a limited economy, poor public education, and poverty. In addition, 64% of Fijian women report experiencing sexual violence from an intimate partner.

Despite these dire statistics, there is hope. Recent attention to catcalling, street violence, rape, and dating violence is triggering a response from some politicians, both in the United States and abroad. While this movement is slow, it is vital that activists of all genders join together to stop sexual violence and street harassment around the world.

In addition, rape is frequently used as a means of genocide in conflicts between warring groups of people as a tactic of war. In this instance, rape of the opposition's womenfolk leads to two different outcomes desirable to the perpetrators' side. First, the women who have been raped are frequently seen as contaminated, and many women are rejected from their own homes, if they are lucky enough to have a surviving spouse or parent.

Second, if there is a pregnancy caused by the rape, the resulting child is 50% of the opponent's genetics, producing a mixed group of children who have no home in either country; these children are often rejected by their maternal families, and their paternal families are largely unknown. Either way, the rapists win. They demoralize the womenfolk of their enemy and cause familial strife for people lucky enough to survive.

12. What is stalking? What is cyberstalking?

Strictly speaking, stalking is an old-fashioned term from hunting wild animals. In hunting, it means to cautiously approach one's prey without their knowledge. We can see this most commonly when cats stalk birds. In more modern terms, however, it means to surreptitiously follow someone without their knowledge, acquiring knowledge of their habits, and if the victim were to know about it, they would typically feel fearful or threatened. Stalking is more common than many of us might think, given that a Justice Department study found that 14 of every 1,000 people experienced stalking during the time period covered. The victim of stalking is most often a cisgender female and her stalker a cisgender male; females were stalked at a rate of 20 per 1,000, while males were stalked at a rate of 7 per 1,000. In addition, young people aged eighteen through twenty-four years old are most likely to be stalked. Being stalked by strangers is relatively uncommon at 1 in every 10; 3 out of every 4 stalking victims previously knew their stalker. Most victims identified their stalkers as former intimate partners, former roommates, or neighbors.

There are some common themes in stalking and ways you can determine whether you or a friend or family member is being stalked. First, do you frequently bump into the same person at the same time? Do you then run into that person again in another context or location? For example, when you leave school, do you see someone from one of your classes when you are at the gym or grocery store? While some of these are certainly mere coincidences, if there is a repeated pattern, you should consider the real possibility that you are being stalked. Next, are you being watched by someone? Is someone asking friends or neighbors about you? Is someone taking photos of you while you are unaware? If you see a person repeatedly and they are not where you expect them to be, they may be being stalking you. Next, repeated phone calls from someone you only know casually may be a concern: several calls in one week can be enough to suggest caution in regard to this person. Then, if you suddenly begin receiving gifts from someone who does not know you well, or at all, you may be a victim of stalking. Know that if this happens and they are spurned or rejected, their gifts may escalate and become pornographic or threatening. There are some stalkers who like to "rescue" their victims, either by causing a situation where the victim needs rescuing (e.g., flat tire, "lost" keys) or by coincidentally being there when the victim needs some help (e.g., it is raining and they offer an umbrella). While some of this is merely polite behavior, if it is consistent or more than once, you should be alert to the possibility you are being stalked.

Some stalkers like to manipulate their victims into responding, perhaps by filing meaningless lawsuits against you or threatening to harm themselves or others if you do not interact with them. Other stalkers follow your activity on social media and send unsolicited pictures or links to sites that you have not asked for. Frequently, this is used in tandem with in-person stalking. You can report this activity to your Internet service provider and local law enforcement. Other stalkers try to separate you from your family and friends, often by causing unnecessary harm to a person's reputation; this is so that the stalker can swoop in and provide that comforting shoulder to cry on. Other stalkers threaten violence or break into cars or apartments in an attempt to garner more information about you. You should report this activity to the police, as it may help them track down the stalker and stop them. The final sign that someone may be stalking you is the frequency of the contact between you and an otherwise stranger. Some of this can certainly be chalked up to coincidence, but if you feel concerned or alarmed, you should consider the possibility that you are being stalked.

13. How common are false charges of rape and dating violence?

While there is significant media attention to false charges of rape and dating violence, there is little statistical evidence to support this attention. In fact, rape and dating violence are more often *underreported* rather than falsely reported. In fact, only 8%–10% of women who are raped report their rape to the police, according to studies of female college students. This means that at least 90% of instances of rape and dating violence are *not* reported. Of the few cases that are reported, only 3%–5% of the charges are eventually considered false, but that does not mean that the accusation is made-up or fictitious; there are other reasons why a woman would file a complaint with local authorities and then retract the accusation. She may want to put the whole incident behind her, or she is reluctant to be involved in a police investigation, or she finds that the police investigating her case are perpetuating the stigma surrounding sexual assault. The police themselves may make a mistake in the case by never interviewing the rapist, not following up with potential witnesses, or losing biological or other evidence.

Some studies have found that the police encourage victims to withdraw charges by using intimidation and coercion. They might tell the victim to think about the perpetrator: "You wouldn't want something bad to happen to him, would you?" If he has a family, they might say, "You wouldn't want to mess that up, would you?" Or if he is a star athlete with a chance of becoming a professional athlete, they might say, "You wouldn't want to deprive him of that, would you?" Any of these sorts of coercion are inappropriate and contribute to the likelihood that most men who commit rape will never face charges.

Historically, rape charges have typically been infrequently brought against men, especially men in power or men of influence in their communities. The advent of the #MeToo movement has shifted this dynamic, as more and more people come forward with stories of their own sexual assault, sexual harassment, or rape at the hands of the powerful. However, ideas about women and the propriety of women speaking about sexual assault, harassment, and rape likely decreased the number of women who did report their experience through legal channels. While there were definitely class differences involved in bringing charges, and a perception that the well-to-do were perhaps more libertine in their pursuit of the unwilling, the truth is that women were then as now more likely to be victimized by someone they already knew. Similarly, women of the lower social classes were typically seen as less chaste and more sexually available to men of every social class; a claim of rape from a lower-class woman was likely viewed as part of a plot to wrangle money out of him or his wealthy family. Similarly, women of color have historically been seen as less chaste, older than they actually are, and more sexually available to men of every race or social class. This leads to a perception that young people of color are much older than they actually are, leading to heightened sexual attention and more intensive policing activities. This falsehood is perpetuated in a media environment that suggests chastity is a behavioral element only for the white and well-to-do.

Part of the reason it is so difficult to put an exact number on charges of rape that are ultimately deemed false is that the data does not take into account those cases that are deemed positive but not provable in a court of law—a much higher standard than the facts might suggest. Indeed, the Philadelphia Police Department was found to have "dumped" cases to reduce workload for a period of over twenty years. These victims, despite having done what we are all told to do—file a police report, see a medical health professional, and provide evidence—were denied their day in court. It should be noted that cases that are unfounded are often unprosecutable for other reasons but are believed to have had a real sexual assault, rape, or dating violence incident behind them. A case can be considered unfounded if the victim did not sustain visible or internal injuries, the rapist did not use force or a weapon, the rapist and the victim have a history of sexual intercourse, there is a lack of physical evidence, or there are inconsistencies between the victim's account and other verifiable evidence.

Another reason a person might withdraw a rape charge or a dating violence charge is because of the social status of their attacker. If the attacker is a well-known celebrity or part of an established or wealthy family, the victim may feel that her charge will bring her, her family, or her community a great deal of scrutiny and shame. This is despite the common thought that women who do file charges against the wealthy or a celebrity are merely gold digging. In addition, even if a rape victim brings charges against their attacker that does not mean that the local district attorney will choose to prosecute the case—another layer that can lead to the perception that false rape charges are common. However, district attorneys are scrupulously concerned with their conviction-to-acquittal ratio, as that is used as an indicator of their effectiveness in enforcing the law. Therefore, district attorneys represent the final gatekeepers for cases to be brought to court, or not, and they frequently decline to press charges in cases of rape where any evidence might be murky or questionable.

Somewhere between 6% and 38% of men report behavior that is sexually coercive, while many more have engaged in behaviors in public or private that would reach the level of sexual harassment, sexual assault, or rape. The sad truth is that many men in the United States see nothing wrong with groping a woman at a party or a bar or grinding against a stranger on the dance floor. While most of these men might now be ashamed of this behavior and would be horrified if it were ever known, or would be outraged if this happened to the women they care about, the sad truth is that our society does little to demonstrate to men, young and old, that this behavior is undesirable, abhorrent, and socially unacceptable.

According to one study, men are much more likely to become victims of rape rather than be falsely accused of rape. This study found that a man is 230 times more likely to be raped than to be falsely accused of rape. The unfortunate fact is that if you or a loved one is accused of rape or dating violence, serious consideration must be given to the statistical likelihood that a rape or dating violence incident did occur, regardless of how much that you or that other person protests or how much you care for them.

While there may be a public perception that rape is the most frequently falsely charged crime, the data does not support that perception. Of overturned convictions, false convictions for murder outnumber false convictions for rape or attempted rape.

Purposely false charges of rape tend to be lurid, with unnecessary cruelty being a common element. Part of the reason for this is that the person who makes up false rape charges is desperate to be believed, and they believe these dramatic and cruel details make their charge more plausible, at least at first, and tend to elicit sympathy from the people hearing the story. None of the studies found that people with a mental illness, including depression, bipolar disorder, and anxiety, are more likely to make false charges; indeed, people with mental illness are more likely to be victims of rape rather than to file false charges. The thought that women cry rape after sex with a less-than-ideal partner is also common, but the facts do not support this theory either. The term for this is *postcoital regret*, but most people who bring rape charges do so because they were raped rather than because they regret having had sex with someone. In all instances, it is safer to assume that someone who claims to have been raped or sexually assaulted is telling the truth; statistically, it is the most likely reason for their claim.

Causes, Consequences, and Prevention of Rape and Dating Violence

14. What causes dating violence?

While there is only one true cause of dating violence, a person who is out of control emotionally, there are societal factors that make this phenomenon a more frequent occurrence. One reason may be that some people believe that violence, whether it is domestic or dating, is a normal part of life; it is unfortunate but completely acceptable, or at least understandable, when it happens. Another reason might be that the aggressor is angry, anxious, depressed, fearful, or has some other emotional trauma that has not been thoroughly processed. The aggressor may believe that dating violence is normal because they grew up in a domestically violent household—that is, violence with a significant other is familiar and, in some skewed way, comforting. In addition, an early advent of sexual activity along with having had a number of sexual partners may increase the risk of dating violence, as can having a friend who is also in a violent dating relationship. In addition, the use of drugs or alcohol can also lower one's inhibitions and make the unthinkable, striking one's partner, seem reasonable. Some theorists posit that dating or domestic violence occurs when a partner is enraged or otherwise emotionally triggered at work and cannot express their emotions there for fear of losing their job. For rape, a similar sort of mindset is likely at play; coercive sex is seen as overcoming the victim's opposition rather than what it truly is: sexual assault or rape. This idea of a conquest mentality, or the number of people one has sex with, ensures that dating or domestic violence, sexual assault, and rape have a continued presence in our lives.

Another reason for dating violence is that young people are still working on developing the skills involved in romantic relationships. Theoretically, as they mature, their dating and relationship skills will also develop. For many people, there are no good role models for how healthy intimate relationships should work, and the media does not help with this problem. From romance novels, commonly known as "bodice rippers"; to stalking situations in numerous films; to television programs, including telenovelas, media does a poor job of showing healthy relationships to young people. In addition, young people may not feel comfortable communicating their feelings with their partners, or they may ineffectively communicate because their family members never talked about their feelings, or they may be misunderstood, either purposely or inadvertently, by their partner. In addition, a person may use threats or violence to get their way, as a way to express their frustration or anger, or simply because they know no other way to act. In addition, hanging out with violent friends can lead to a belief that violence is no big deal or not a problem. A lack of parental support or supervision can also lead to the sense that dating violence is not a big deal or should not be seen as a problem. Young people with strong family support or a sense of community are among the least likely to find themselves in relationships that include dating violence.

Male sexual jealousy of their partner is also a frequent precursor to domestic or dating violence. Furthermore, people who are violent with their intimate partner typically wait until there is some sort of emotional commitment between them and their victim; this can include committing to a monogamous dating relationship, having sex for the first time, moving in together, or becoming engaged or pregnant, whether planned or not. It seems that the greater emotional connection triggers some people into believing they have a right to control their partner's behavior, as if their partner and their partner's identity are now intertwined with the identity of the batterer or rapist.

As one might expect, dealing with mental health issues can also tend toward dating violence, although people with mental illness are most frequently the targets of domestic or dating violence. Having a learning disability is another contributing factor in some cases, although learning disabilities do not preclude happy and successful relationships. Peer pressure to engage in behaviors one might not engage in otherwise can lead to dating violence, as can exposure to violent content in films, videos, and music. While films, videos, and music do not cause violence per se, they do tend to make violence seem more acceptable. Having a history of bullying, either as a victim or as a bully, increases the risk of dating violence. Seeing unhealthy relationships glamorized online, or heard in music, may cause young people to think that violence is a normal part of healthy adult relationships when that is not true.

People from families who are experiencing other sorts of turbulence, such as financial issues, the separation of parents, problems with addictive behaviors, or rigid stereotypical gender roles, may face an increased risk of engaging in dating or domestic violence, either as the aggressor or the victim. The frustration of these situations and a lack of clear communication can pave the way for misunderstandings that quickly escalate to physically, verbally, or sexually violent incidents. Low-income families face struggles that may lead to frustration, anger, and emotional distress that may lead to instances of intimate partner violence, dating violence, or domestic violence, although people from middle-class and upper-class families find themselves in domestically violent situations too. In addition, people in the Latinx and Black communities face three to four times more dating violence than their white peers, while Asian Americans have the least likelihood of being in violent dating or domestic relationships.

Engaging in other delinquent behavior, such as running away from home; smoking cigarettes or vaping, whether tobacco or otherwise; skipping school; gambling; or other illicit behavior, increases the risks for dating violence. If both partners are involved in delinquent behavior, the risk of dating violence increases too. In addition, dating a partner who is significantly older can lead to an increase in the risk of dating violence.

Given that relationships occur as much online as they do face to face, it is no surprise that dating violence leaks into online relationships too. In the case of online dating violence, stalking, hacking, tracking via geo-locators, making false accusations of infidelity or other things, playing the victim, encouraging others to harass the victim, ordering embarrassing products that are then sent to the victim's home or workplace, harassing the victim on social media sites, posing as another person on a dating app, and posting revenge porn are common reactions to rejection for some attackers. Cyberstalking is a crime that is more and more frequent: one out of twelve women and one out of forty-five men have been victims of cyberstalking. Cyberstalkers tend to be male, as 87% of all cyberstalking is done by men, and women are much more likely to be victims of cyberstalking, as four out of five cyberstalking victims are female. This particular crime is receiving attention at the local, state, and federal levels. Some cases are being handed over to the U.S. district attorney by the FBI, and others are sent to the state's attorney general. If you believe you or a friend is being cyberstalked, please refer to the additional resources part of this book for more information about dealing with this pernicious problem.

Historically speaking, dating or domestic violence was typical in most relationships. Prior to women and children being seen as more than property, in the mid-1800s, beating and screaming at a dependent, whether wife, child, or slave, was believed to be instructive; that is, the beating or screaming was to "correct" the behavior that had been found problematic, typically by a male head of household. It was as if the violence, whether physical or verbal, was meant to discipline the other person. In more recent history, domestic violence was a commonplace in many American households. It was not until the 1960s that women were able to open their own bank accounts, and opening a credit card in their own name was not legal until 1974; prior to that, a woman was thought to be dependent on the male head of household—her father or her husband—and so she did not need her own bank account or credit card. In addition, the infantilization of modern women also leads to a sense that screaming at or beating them is "for their own good" rather than what is actually is: aggression against someone who is likely physically weaker.

Some theorists believe that domestic or dating violence is a manifestation of a lack of agency on the part of the aggressor, either in the workplace or in their educational or other community setting. The significant other is seen as a safe space to vent these frustrations, and they typically receive this abuse in a predictable pattern. The abuse often happens prior to their significant other going to school or work or afterward. These bursts of violent action are typically followed by a period of contrition, promises to never allow it to happen again, and attempts to make peace with the victim.

15. What causes rape?

The obvious and simple answer for what causes rape is rapists, but there is more to it than that. For one, we live in a culture where some people's appearances are deemed more important than their intellect, philanthropy, experience, or ability. This, along with misogynistic and homophobic language and images, leads to what is known as *rape culture*, or the sense that rape is pervasive, and denies women and folks in the LGBTQIA+ community, both cisgender and trans, agency or control over their own bodies and ignores their basic human right to bodily integrity and self-determination. Because of the prevalence of rape culture in American society, many women, young girls, and folks in the LGBTQIA+ community modify or restrict their behavior to avoid situations that might put them in greater danger. This sort of avoidance of danger is typically invisible or unknown to cisgender straight males. One person's rape is a tragedy for them but acts as an implicit warning to other people—that rape is what happens when people do not follow gendered norms or have the temerity to think or speak for themselves. In this way, rape culture holds cisgender straight men as superior and keeps everyone else as their subordinates in perpetuity.

Part of rape culture is the insistence on dress codes for young women so they do not "distract" young men in the classroom, rather than teaching young men that women are not sexual objects who are there for their titillation; street harassment, such as catcalling; and misogynistic language and images used in advertisements. Rape culture also insists on teaching women how to stay safe while ignoring the real fact that men are typically the ones doing the raping and should be taught to ask for positive consent every step of the way during any sexual activity.

While rape culture is one contributor to rape, what is more important is that our society tends to treat romantic relationships in a skewed manner. First, we talk about the people we have sex with as if they are objects to be won or lost, conquests, or as if sexual relations are a game rather than seeing potential partners as individuals who are worthy of love and affection. The idea of scoring a win by having sex with someone confirms this perception. Second, doing this dehumanizes the partner and makes it easier to act in a sexually violent way; after all, if they are hardly human or merely a number, where is the harm? Third, in our society, people speak about other people in terms of their body parts, as if the rest of them does not exist. We can see this most clearly in the comments frequently heard coming from people who catcall. If women are typically valued for their sexuality, then a man who has sex with a woman is deemed better for having had sex with her while she herself is diminished in terms of her reputation or her value in society. This is also an element of rape culture—that women who have sex are deemed less than or damaged goods—that is, if the sexual activity occurs outside of marriage.

Men who have trouble finding intimate partners or who feel that there is something missing in their intimate relationship show some predisposition to rape and other violent behavior. This includes those who consider themselves involuntarily celibate, or an incel, as they call themselves; these people believe that they have a right to sex, typically with women, and that the people who will not date them are all less than human, thus making violence against them not only a legitimate response but very nearly required and frequently in a corrective manner, as if they are trying to teach such people a lesson. The problem with this way of thinking is that their very attitude ensures that no one with any sort of people skills will want to have sex with them, thus creating a paradoxically self-fulfilling prophecy.

The problem with rape culture and rigid gender roles is that it denies the existence of people who are gender nonconforming, or members of the LGBTQIA+ community. If rigid gender roles are the expectation, then bullying, taunting, and shaming those who are gender nonconforming, gay, or lesbian becomes the norm as well as a way for heteronormative people to assert their own heterosexuality or to displace their anxiety about their own sexual identity onto a group that they deem safe to attack. Women who act or dress too femininely are punished, as are women who do not act or dress femininely at all. A similar idea is true for men; those who act or dress in a more masculine manner are glorified, while those who do not are frequently accused of being gay. Either way, cisgender heteronormativity is seen as preferable and dominant. This is known as heteronormative sexuality, and it imposes strict gender roles on all of us and leads to a culture where rape works as one of the ways to control people who do not fall into line with rigid gender expectations.

In addition, victim blaming and ignoring the ways in which masculinity is harmful, or toxic, contribute to a culture where consent is ignored or cannot be given and sexual activity occurs nonetheless. Our culture glamorizes violence and aggression and then acts surprised when young people imitate what they have seen and heard through media or elsewhere. Violence in intimate relationships is about power dynamics. Men who rape are typically not in a rapturous state when they rape (the literal meaning of *rape* is related to this concept); rather, they are exerting their power over someone who either has not or cannot consent to sexual activity. Masculinity does not have to be this way. It is possible to be a heterosexual, homosexual, or gender nonconforming male or female and to care about the person one wants to have sex with. One way to ensure that a person is not accused of rape is to employ what is known as enthusiastic consent; the person frequently checks in with their partner to ensure that everything of a sexual nature that happens between them is 100% consensual. Partners need to work on being able to describe what they like and do not like in a sexual encounter to maximize pleasure for both partners and to help everyone develop healthy relationships with their sexual partners.

Many men who rape do not think of their behavior as being rape; instead, they join our culture in blaming the victim or think so highly of themselves that the idea that they could have raped someone is inconceivable. Men who rape typically begin early, in high school or the early years of college; those with greater empathy are less likely to repeat the act and likely feel shame when recalling the act, while those who lack empathy tend to continue raping and harming more and more people. Many men might reveal that they have had sex that they coerced, and yet they do not think of this as an act of rape. Instead, most men think of rape as something abhorrent and would be mortified if a sexual partner were to suggest that their encounter was nonconsensual, or rape. Rather, they think of rape and rapists as something that other men do, particularly bad men, and not themselves or their friends. The damage that this knowledge could cause a man makes looking too closely at past sexual relationships psychologically dangerous territory indeed.

The problem is that all of the advice given to women tends to suggest that if you follow the steps, you will avoid being raped, implying that someone else who does not follow the steps or guidelines as precisely as you do will be raped. This is about as dark a piece of advice as a person can think of—save yourself by shifting this pain and trauma to someone else. The trouble is that rapists are not doing this because of what a person wears, drinks, eats, or any other behavior; rather, they do it as an expression of their dominance and desire to dehumanize their victim. It is a manifestation of the misogyny in our culture more broadly and is unfortunately written on the bodies of victims every day. Victims of rape can be as young as infants or as old as nursing home residents. What matters is that if there is no consent to the sexual activity, it is rape.

16. What is the cycle of abuse?

The cycle of abuse is a visual representation of the emotional states that happen between partners in a violent dating or domestic relationship over and over again. Lenore E. Walker first introduced the concept after working with survivors of domestic violence. Walker noticed that there were common elements to these dysfunctional relationships, and she used these elements to create a graphic representation of the cycle of battering, later called a cycle of abuse to include other sorts of domestic or dating violence and victims other than cisgender, straight women.

The beginning of the violent dating or domestic relationship is frequently like a fairy tale, as the soon-to-be abuser charms the intended victim. There is a sense that the budding relationship is too good to be true as the course of the relationship quickly crosses boundaries that a normal relationship would cross much later. The soon-to-be victim may feel as if they have been swept off their feet as their new love interest does everything in their power to charm them into a relationship. Intimacy is frequently an early feature of the relationship, and that emotional commitment may be enough to trigger an emotionally violent response to some small stimulus.

The next phase of the cycle is the isolation of the victim through lies or other emotional manipulation. The abuser tells the victim that their friends are not good for them or that the victim's friends hate the abuser and insists that the victim break off relationships with them. If it is the victim's family raising the red flags, the abuser tells the victim that only they understand them and that their family just wants the victim to remain a child or is using them for other reasons, including babysitting younger siblings or for their economic contributions to the household. Whatever the lie is, the common theme is that the abuser is the only one that the victim needs to rely on, as the abuser is the only one who really knows the victim best.

Once the victim is isolated from friends and family, tension between the abuser and victim increases. The abuser may threaten violence to the victim or to people or things the victim loves, including pets or family members. Verbal abuse is common at this stage, and the victim adjusts their behavior in the mistaken belief that doing so will help them avoid additional outbursts. Eventually, all of these efforts prove futile, and the abuser breaks into physically violent behavior or the threat of physically violent behavior. Whether this involves punching, slapping, kicking, choking, or otherwise hurting their partner, it is never the victim's fault, although the abuser will insist that if the victim proved their love more fully by doing exactly what they require, exactly when they require it, then the abuser would not have these violent outbursts. Frequently, the abuser will claim that they are the victim of their beloved's lack of respect for them or their needs, rather than owning their violence as a response that comes only from them and their behaviors.

The last phase of the cycle is known as the honeymoon phase, as the elation of the courtship is repeated to ensure that the victim stays with the abuser. The abuser promises to never have a violent outburst again and plies their victim with those things that the victim likes, even if these things are things the abuser previously denied the victim (especially true in cases of food control, money control, or isolation from friends or family). The abuser likely makes an earnest effort to control their violent tendencies, but without therapy, a good deal of personal reflection, and a desire to change, nothing will change. Instead, tensions will inevitably begin to build again, a period frequently described as walking on eggshells, as the victim knows that there is increasing tension and tries to avoid another physically violent event.

If therapy and a desire to change are not happening, if there is a denial that there is a problem, or, at worst, if the abuser continues to blame the victim for the violent outbursts, the best thing a victim can do is to try to leave the abuser. However, this also presents a number of challenges. Some victims who live with their abusers have turned over control of their finances to the abuser and will have no money to live on if they leave. Others have been kept at home to take care of the abuser's household or children and so have no financial resources or an employment history that will help them find a job more easily. Others yet have been prevented from taking jobs, so they have few skills that might bring in an income. And some victims have been encouraged to drop out of school, further limiting their ability to find employment. Furthermore, leaving a violent dating or domestic situation is the most dangerous time of a victim's life: 70% of domestic violence partners who are murdered are murdered when they try to leave their abuser.

Escaping a domestically violent situation is even more imperative if there are children involved, as children who witness violence in the home are much more likely to become involved in violent relationships of their own, as either an abuser or a victim, once they are adults and begin their own intimate relationships. There is some evidence that children growing up in domestically violent households show signs of psychological disturbance or emotional issues that manifest at school or other safe spaces when there is little threat of the abuser catching them. Sometimes this shows up in schools as bullying other students, as the child who has witnessed violence in the household tries to act similar to their abusive parent, perhaps as a means of regaining some control over their own lives that the abuser has taken from them.

17. What are the short- and long-term physical consequences of dating violence?

There are numerous consequences of dating violence, some obvious and some not so obvious. In the short-term, dating violence may cause the victim to suffer broken bones, bruises, internal injuries, vaginal bleeding or pelvic pain, unwanted pregnancies, sexually transmitted diseases, or nightmares or trouble sleeping. There are also long-term potential impacts on a victim's health, including arthritis, asthma, chronic pain, digestive issues (including irritable bowel syndrome), heart problems, migraines, sexual issues during intercourse (including an inability to climax or become aroused), immunological disorders, lack of engagement or diminished interest in academic success, a greater tendency toward suicidal ideation, or increasing incidents of self-harm.

In addition, victims of dating or domestic violence typically withdraw from their family and friends to appease their abuser's demand for 100% of the victim's time and attention. This isolation can lead to the victim losing their self-confidence and becoming fearful of expressing emotions, as this can be a source for a potential blowup, and can include physical injuries up to and unfortunately including their own death.

In the longer term, victims of dating violence may find themselves feeling a plethora of negative emotions, from shame, guilt, loneliness, or embarrassment to PTSD, or they may develop an inability to form lasting healthy relationships with another partner. Other victims may find themselves self-medicating with alcohol, tobacco, or other substances in an attempt to avoid the negative feelings they have become accustomed to. In addition, some victims may begin bullying or hitting other people, stealing, or lying to people to get their way. In addition, students who were victimized in high school find themselves more likely to be victimized in their intimate relationships in college. Females who experience dating violence are more likely to suffer from depression and are more likely to binge drink or smoke cigarettes, suffer from eating disorders, or engage in risky sexual behaviors. They are less likely to use condoms during sexual activity and are more likely to use marijuana. In addition, six months after admitting dating violence, victims reported more mental health issues and substance dependency. It must be said that admitting the violent relationship does not cause the mental health issues or substance dependency; rather, it is an outcome of the violent relationship itself. It is somewhat likely that those who admit that their relationship was violent also find themselves more introspective and aware of their emotions and behaviors than those who continue the relationship without the admission that the relationship is violent.

These effects are magnified if the young adult lacks models of healthy adult romantic relationships; that is, if the victim comes from a domestically violent household, the impact of dating violence is greater on them, as violence in intimate relationships can be seen as somewhat normal and perhaps oddly comforting and familiar. If the media is the only place where a young person learns how to be in an intimate relationship, there is likely to be trouble in their relationships, as media-presented relationships only focus on the high or low spots of a relationship, and these are far more dramatic than the everyday nature of most relationships. To be sure, there is nothing normal about dating violence, and parents, teachers, doctors, nurses, and other adults in young people's lives have to do a better job of educating them about healthy relationships and harmful behaviors.

In some states, such as California, a young person in a violent dating relationship may be prosecuted for that violence and may end up on a domestic violence offender or sex offender registry, thus impacting their future educational, career, or other long-term goals. Likewise, California allows teens in violent relationships to take out restraining orders against their abuser; in fact, children as young as twelve years old are able to request a restraining order from a judge without the knowledge of a parent or guardian, although many judges may find it necessary to inform a parent. While these laws help young people in California, we should all be advocating for similar legislation where we live. This would be a great activity for a group of high school or college-aged students to advocate for, as this is the only way changes happen to the legal system. A fraternity- or sorority-led effort might achieve great success in advocating for victims of dating violence and bringing about changes to the legal system.

18. What are the short- and long-term physical consequences of rape?

The short-term physical consequences of rape include soreness, bleeding, difficulty walking, painful intercourse, urinary tract infections, pregnancy, sexually transmitted disease(s), and potentially uterine fibroids. During the assault or rape, the victim's body releases stress hormones in response to the trauma; this is the body's attempt to reduce pain and inflammation, and it raises blood sugars, perhaps in an attempt to prepare to flee the situation. In addition, there is a higher likelihood of experiencing high blood pressure, higher triglycerides, and sleep issues. Because of trust issues, some victims find themselves avoiding going to the dentist or the doctor, as each of these relationships involves a level of trust and vulnerability.

There is also some evidence that there are long-term increased risks for coronary artery disease, as the body's response to stress, whether immediate or remembered, releases hormones that increase heart rate and prepare the body to take flight. There is evidence that the stress of sexual assault or rape deregulates the body's stress responses, leading to a cascade of physical ailments. The degree to which a person realizes these impacts is affected by their social support at the time of the assault or rape; people with stronger social support appear to escape many of the more serious long-term consequences. Regardless of your social support, it is imperative to deal with the emotional toll of sexual assault or rape, at least as much for your physical well-being as well as for your mental health.

While not technically physical, there are psychological effects that affect a victim's well-being, including PTSD, depression, and anxiety; trouble connecting with a significant other or romantic partner; flashbacks (a memory of the rape as if it is happening again right now); eating disorders, including anorexia, bulimia, and binge eating and purging; feeling guilt or blaming oneself for what happened; self-mutilation or other self-destructive behaviors; distrust of others; anger; feeling as if sex does not really matter and engaging in a lot of meaningless sex; feeling powerless, weak, or vulnerable; feeling a lack of control of one's own body; or, somewhat less likely, dissociative identity disorder (the development of one or more alternate personalities with or without the victim's awareness).

There is some evidence to suggest that people who experience rape as a young person tend to engage in promiscuous sexual activity or risky sex with other people, tend to use or abuse drugs and alcohol, and tend to do more poorly in academic settings. In addition, victims often find themselves impoverished, as they either leave the home where they were victimized (in the case of rape or sexual assault by a family member) or leave their abuser, frequently without financial support from family members who might otherwise have provided support. Poverty is particularly likely if the rape occurs between people who work together, as victims may find themselves punished for bringing the rape to the attention of their manager or human resources personnel or fired if it was the victim's manager who committed the rape. On the other hand, some victims find that they lose all interest in sexual activity or have a reduced or nonexistent desire for sexual encounters in the future. Many victims find that they are more likely to experience PTSD during foreplay or coitus because they relive the trauma from their victimization. In addition, those victims who desire sex less frequently may also find that their enjoyment of sexual activity diminishes as well.

If the rapist is an intimate partner, this complicates the short- and long-term effects of the rape. Unsurprisingly, these relationships frequently break up or end within six months of the rape. Issues regarding self-worth, self-confidence, and self-esteem are particularly impacted when the rapist is an intimate partner; victims may experience depression, anxiety, sexual dysfunction, or eating disorders. Family members may shun the victim, or the victim may feel humiliated, ashamed, or guilty, especially in cases where the rapist is also an intimate partner.

Given that rape typically happens between people who know one another (only about 10% of rapes are perpetrated by a stranger), the social network that both the victim and the rapist share will be impacted. Typically, the victim's future ability to attract a partner may be diminished, but the rapist peculiarly seems to suffer no negative impact, as they and their friends and family most frequently do not believe that the act was rape in the first place, or blame the victim, or chalk it all up to a misunderstanding or the mental instability of the victim. The rapist's sense of self as a good person is not damaged, while the victim's sense of self as a good person is called into question by the very same act, and notably through no fault of the victim. In addition, this sort of dynamic can include elements of so-called slut-shaming, which involves blaming the victim for what happened, blaming the victim for reporting it, or blaming the victim for ruining the rapist's life, whether in person or on social media. The simple truth is that when a person claims to have been raped, statistically speaking, they likely were raped. As a society, we would do well to listen to rape victims when they bring forward charges of rape.

19. What happens if a woman becomes pregnant as a result of rape?

Similar to other instances of unplanned pregnancies, there are a variety of results, although rape as a cause of an unplanned pregnancy is more nuanced and perhaps more emotionally charged. Surprisingly, pregnancy as an effect of rape is more common than currently perceived by most people. In addition to the normal hormonal changes in mood, pregnancy as a result of rape causes challenges to a woman's sense of self, health, and well-being. It is suggested that the risk of pregnancy as a result of rape should be approximately 4%–10%, but startling data from wartime rapes and pregnancies suggest something closer to 70%, as conceptions happened outside of the normally fertile periods. There are medical professionals studying the phenomenon who theorize that the act of rape itself triggers ovulation; therefore, conception occurs at higher rates than during consensual sex. Rape has frequently been a tool used by the military to further divide their enemy. Many women raped by an invading army are rejected by their own families, and if they are unlucky enough to become pregnant, their children are 50% the child of the enemy, with no hope of finding a father to provide support and no extended family to help with child-rearing.

In abusive relationships, sexual activity that is coerced nearly guarantees a pregnancy as a result of rape if birth control is unavailable or inconsistently used or if the woman is prevented from using birth control by her abusive partner. An abused woman's sense of autonomy in an abusive relationship that also coerces sexual activity may mean that the expectant mother fails to seek proper medical care, whether or not the pregnancy is otherwise desirable. It is currently estimated that over 32,000 pregnancies each year are due to rape. One of the major complications of pregnancy due to rape occurs because many victims do not discover their pregnancy until they enter the second trimester, when their options for dealing with the unwanted pregnancy have narrowed in many states. This is especially true for those victims who refuse or are denied access to medical care after their victimization by their abuser.

In fact, denial of birth control in abusive relationships is frequently a precursor to an unintended pregnancy, as the abuser seeks to maintain authority over the victim and deny her autonomy, or the right to determine the course of her life, take charge of her own finances, her own desire, and the intervals between children. Taken one step further, the victim becoming pregnant is potentially part of the plan, whether consciously or subconsciously, on the part of the abuser. If the victim is pregnant or has children with her abuser, it is much more difficult for her to leave him and seek a healthy relationship and her own destiny. Additionally, custody issues ensure that the abuser will always be in his victim's life, even frequently despite a conviction for rape. However, for all women who have an unplanned pregnancy, there are essentially three options: carry the pregnancy to term and keep the baby, carry the pregnancy to term and give the baby up for adoption, or choose an abortion. In the case of abortion, these are best done during the first trimester, when there is less at risk for the mother's health, and there are more options available to women who live in states that otherwise restrict access to abortion, depending on how far along the pregnancy is. These choices are never made lightly. Every woman who faces these choices is under a lot of pressure, but women who are pregnant as a result of rape face additional burdens.

Feelings of grief and loss are fairly common for women who become pregnant as a result of rape, particularly when their rapist is someone with whom they have been intimate in the past. Attachment to the fetus as it develops is more challenging for these mothers, as they may face an inability to separate their feelings regarding the act that caused the pregnancy and the resulting pregnancy. Furthermore, the invasive procedures required by the medical community during pregnancy may trigger flashbacks, seemingly excessive emotions, or other PTSD-like effects. However, many mothers who choose to complete their pregnancy find that once they see their newborn, they see the baby as a separate person from their attacker rather than a manifestation of rape; in these cases, maternal bonds are typically formed, and the relationship can be healthy, although not every mother-child relationship works out this way. One of the major reasons for this sort of bonding and healthy relationship between the mother and child is because the society around the pregnant mother accepted and encouraged her during her pregnancy. Unsupportive statements or behaviors from her social circle appear to lead to more negative outcomes regarding maternal bonding and the health of the mother-child bond. The number one thing that a woman pregnant against her will needs to hear is that she is supported and will be taken care of rather than be excluded from her family or social groups, which happens all too frequently, particularly in strictly religious or traditional households.

It should be noted that pregnancy, whether by rape or by consensual sex, is a dangerous time for women, as dating or domestic violence tends to escalate during this period. This violence can lead to complications in the pregnancy or, in extreme cases, to the death of the fetus or mother. In cases of intimate partner rape, a safety plan should be developed so that the mother feels she has a place or people to go to if things escalate. In fact, 25% of intimate partner homicides happen during the first trimester of a victim's pregnancy.

Emergency contraception should be a consideration for all women who find themselves unintentionally pregnant or uncertain about whether they used effective protection during sexual activity. It should be readily available over the counter to anyone for around $40–$50, regardless of age or other considerations. Some women might want to keep emergency contraception on hand in case of accidentally having sex without protection, a failure of their protection, or an intimate partner coercing or forcing them into sex or to have on hand for their friends.

Given that effective birth control has only been widely available in the United States since the early 1960s, and was initially only available to married women, it is likely that this problem was much worse in the past. Women who did not want to continue their unintended pregnancies faced home or back-alley abortions; used other methods to end the pregnancy, including herbs or poultices; or had their children out of wedlock and put them up for adoption. Abortion as we know it now has only been legal since 1974 with the U.S. Supreme Court decision in *Roe v. Wade*;

meanwhile, many states have imposed increasing restrictions on the availability of abortion and who might perform them, with some states going
so far as to criminalize abortion providers and seeking to fine women who
experience miscarriages or otherwise end a pregnancy, wanted or not. The
Supreme Court's overruling of *Roe v. Wade* means that access to abortion
is even more challenging for many women throughout the United States.

20. What are the long-term psychological effects for victims of rape or dating violence?

The long-term psychological effects for victims of rape or dating violence
include a greater risk for depression, anxiety, PTSD, and eating disorders, including bulimia, anorexia, and binge eating; high blood pressure;
insomnia; and dissociation, which is feeling that one is outside of one's
body—all likely due to the stress put on the body and the mind. It is
important to point out that not all victims experience these effects and
that not experiencing these effects does not make your experience less
real or traumatic. For those who do experience effects, it is also important
to note that many of these effects may only be temporary.

The risk for depression for people who experience sexual assault or rape
is about twice what it should otherwise be. This is due to at least two
societal issues: first, we live in a society where it is still challenging to
report sexual assault or rape, and second, those who do report their assault
may find themselves being harshly interrogated and may feel themselves
under attack again. Furthermore, the risk of developing anxiety is greatly
increased for victims of sexual assault or rape, likely due to depression
alongside a concern that one might be victimized again. PTSD, a syndrome with many symptoms, causes victims to relive the assault again and
again and is more frequent after sexual assault or rape, as if the brain and
body are still processing the events of what happened. PTSD symptoms
include nausea, intense sweating, high blood pressure, anxiety, nightmares,
insomnia, a sense of life no longer being normal, disinterest in friends or
activities one used to enjoy, and becoming emotionally numb. Unfortunately, those who do not develop PTSD within a month of the attack are
not immune; some folks develop PTSD within six months or longer after
the attack. Of even greater concern is the potential to develop what is
known as chronic PTSD, which suggests that these symptoms continue
into the victim's foreseeable future.

Eating disordered behavior is a common reaction to rape or dating
violence. Binging, purging, restrictive diets, and overexercising all lead

to the release of neurotransmitters that change the brain's chemistry. Increased dopamine causes the victim to feel better temporarily through this sort of restrictive control. Some folks engage in disordered eating in an attempt to control at least one facet of their lives while everything else feels out of control or chaotic. When rape or dating violence occurs, it is as if everything that is normal and under control has been violently ripped away. Taking extreme control of eating or exercise routines restores some of that feeling of control. The positive feedback from others that people receive for such excessive control provides a positive feedback loop, so the harmful behavior is reinforced and therefore encouraged to continue. Self-blame and the feeling that the person could have avoided the attack if only they had done something differently can also lead to a feeling that they are unworthy of healthy, nutritious food. In addition, eating disorders and extreme exercise programs take up a lot of time and can distract a person from thinking about the attack or processing it emotionally. While it is stressful to obsessively think about food or exercise, it is definitely easier than thinking about the attack and dealing with the emotional aftermath.

High blood pressure as a result of rape or dating violence is more common than previously believed. In fact, women who report being sexually harassed at work face double the risk of high blood pressure in comparison to their nonharassed peers. The results of a study published in 2018 found that women who experienced rape not only had twice the risk of high blood pressure than their peers but also that high blood pressure is a contributing factor in cardiovascular disease, now the leading cause of death for American women, something that comes as a surprise to many American women. This is particularly the case for people who refuse psychological counseling, as the body deals with the trauma when the victim does not want to deal with the complex emotions associated with their victimization. This process, known as somatization, occurs when the body is overwhelmed by emotional turmoil that has not been dealt with. Anxiety as a result of rape is fairly common too, with assault survivors experiencing a twofold increase in anxiety, whether about a subsequent attack, reliving the attack, or simply the health outcomes as a result of the attack. While some of this increased risk may be due to genetics, it is clear that assault, particularly at a young age, is a risk factor for both anxiety and high blood pressure later in life.

Insomnia, or trouble sleeping, is another frequent psychological impact due to sexual assault, rape, or dating violence, although this impact transcends the divide between the body and the psyche. Insomnia is intrinsically related to the anxiety and depression that plague many assault victims, as the brain pumps adrenaline and epinephrine into the body, keeping the victim on high alert and ready to fight, flee, or freeze. The stress of being attacked causes many victims to relive the incident or to have bad dreams, ultimately causing a lack of sleep. This is a fairly common result of trauma, but it adds to the somatic load that the body carries as the victim goes about their daily activities.

Dissociation can be particularly troubling, as it happens at odd moments when someone is stressed. It can leave one feeling as if their vision is impaired or narrowed, feel like a constriction in the throat, and can lead to concern that they might black out or faint. This feeling of not being in one's body, or not in control of one's body, can occur while the assault is happening, when the victim is near the attacker, or later, seemingly out of nowhere, as the body continues processing what has happened.

While all of these issues are of concern, one way, and perhaps the only way, to alleviate their impact is to seek counseling to deal with the emotional and psychological aftermath of the attack. There are no guarantees, but it appears that adequate, effective counseling helps to minimize these negative impacts on the victim's psyche. Unfortunately, ignoring the problem of dating violence or sexual assault will not magically make the impacts go away.

Historically, people who were assaulted during a dating relationship, whether sexual or not, were encouraged to keep it to themselves by their own family or the family of their partner. It has only been within the last fifty to sixty years that there has been increased awareness of these problems along with support for people who find themselves in these situations. In fact, the very first women's shelter for victims of domestic violence opened in 1970; up until that time, there was a perception that these matters were better left for families and religious institutions to deal with despite the overwhelming evidence that that was not working. It is only since the so-called third wave of feminism in the 1990s that these issues have been brought to public attention and resources provided for victims of rape, sexual assault, and domestic and dating violence.

21. What is PTSD?

Post-traumatic stress disorder (PTSD) is the current name for a long-known phenomenon. During World War I, troops who experienced what we would call PTSD were thought to have shell shock, an aftereffect from the munitions fired. Some residue of this meaning remains, given that most people tend to think of PTSD as something that only military personnel experience. What is less well known is that trauma of nearly any sort can cause a PTSD effect, including things like car accidents, a dangerous encounter with a person or animal, and other sorts of accidents (boating, flying, etc.). This means that many people who experience sexual assault, rape, or dating or domestic violence may have symptoms of PTSD.

The *Diagnostic and Statistical Manual of Mental Disorders* (DSM) recognized PTSD in 1980, although there were numerous calls for its existence in the earlier edition prior to that. (It is important to know that the DSM-5 is a catalog of all mental health issues and is used by mental health professionals to help them diagnose patients. It functions by providing checklists to mental health professionals who can then score a person's fitting or not fitting a particular diagnosis.) PTSD is a fairly normal response to a frightening, scary, or dangerous event. Part of why PTSD happens is due to the fight-or-flight response, which should also include freeze as one of the responses for people in a stressful situation.

Most people who experience trauma and deal with the problem immediately have few or no further repercussions. Then again, there are those who experience continued trauma after a scary or dangerous event. Unfortunately, women are twice as likely to experience PTSD after a traumatic event. There are three types of risk factors outside of a traumatic event that may make a person more likely to develop PTSD. These include a potentially genetic predisposition to PTSD, a physical brain system difference that makes a person more likely to experience PTSD, and environmental factors, such as living in a high-stress situation prior to the assault, that make a person more likely to respond to trauma with PTSD.

There are two types of PTSD: short term and long term. In either case, PTSD usually begins within three months or so of the traumatic event but may be delayed for months or years after the traumatic event. Symptoms need to be significant enough to affect normal functioning to be termed PTSD. These may include reexperiencing the traumatic event through flashbacks, dreams, or obtrusive thoughts that revisit the experience; body flashbacks that include the body responding to the threat or pain even though it is no longer there, including an increased heart rate or shortness of breath; emotional flashbacks that include unexplainably intense emotions not related to current events or situations, including unprompted guilt or shame; staying away from triggering events, people, or places, or avoiding thoughts or feelings that are related to the event; hypervigilance in an attempt to prevent future victimization; insomnia that is partially driven by fear and anxiety; and a near-constant muscle tension that leads to pain issues and fatigue; negative thoughts about oneself, as if blaming oneself for the traumatic event; feeling hopeless about the future;

memory problems, including blocking memories of the traumatic event; detached feelings regarding family and friends; loss of interest in activities one previously enjoyed; trouble experiencing positive emotions; feeling emotionally numb; and potentially experiencing suicidal thoughts or feelings. Having PTSD may make a person more likely to suffer other mental illnesses, such as depression, anxiety, issues with drug or alcohol abuse, disordered eating (bulimia, anorexia, and binge eating), suicidal thoughts or feelings, or self-harm.

Long-term PTSD is similar to short-term PTSD except that there is greater likelihood of more serious adverse health effects, such as chronic pain, an increased susceptibility to autoimmune diseases, social isolation and withdrawal, a decreased ability to maintain healthy interpersonal relationships, and a greater likelihood of separation or divorce from a significant other.

Patients with PTSD are typically diagnosed by a medical professional, who will begin with physical and mental examinations and then use the DSM guidelines to determine whether the person does have PTSD. Typically, in the DSM, there is a checklist of symptoms, and a certain number of symptoms indicate that a person does or does not have PTSD per se. Even if you are not diagnosed with PTSD, there is no doubt that you are suffering. There is some evidence that nearly 50% of people who suffer from PTSD or who experience symptoms of PTSD are more likely to abuse drugs or alcohol if they are left untreated.

PTSD is best treated by first acknowledging the trauma that has occurred. Treatment may include psychological counseling and possibly medication to alleviate the more troubling symptoms. Most PTSD therapy includes a cognitive-based approach, such as cognitive behavioral therapy (CBT); this involves teaching the victim to change their thought patterns surrounding the traumatic event. First, victims are invited to talk about the trauma and then write about the trauma; both of these are part of learning to emotionally process through the trauma and move beyond it. Next, victims are exposed to things that remind them of the initial traumatic event, and if these things have been hitherto avoided, this is done with support so that the environment loses its emotionally traumatizing elements. In addition, some PTSD patients have found relief through eye movement desensitization and reprocessing (EMDR), which is utilized alongside exposure therapy with guided eye movements to help them process the traumatic event. Dialectical behavior therapy (DBT) has proven useful for some folks with PTSD, and it includes elements of CBT along with Eastern mindfulness practices and a shift in perspective to allow for multiple perspectives rather than rigid categorizations.

Possible medications include antidepressants to help alleviate symptoms of depression and anxiety, and antianxiety medications are often prescribed to alleviate more severe anxiety symptoms. If medications are prescribed, it is critical to follow the treatment plan; not doing so can lead to relapses or a recurrence of symptoms, including lack of sleep, insomnia, stomach difficulties, panic attacks, or seizures. In addition, people who are diagnosed with PTSD should learn more about the syndrome to work toward coping strategies; take good care of yourself, including avoiding stimulants such as nicotine, caffeine, and depressants such as alcohol or other drugs; break the cycle when you begin to feel anxious by getting up and moving, exercising, or doing something else; and consider joining a support group. In particular, yoga appears to help people with PTSD regain a positive relationship with their bodies; people with PTSD may want to consider developing a regular yoga and meditation practice as part of an ongoing mental health plan.

Unsurprisingly, many film and other media depictions of people with PTSD focus on ex-military personnel, although others focus on traumatic events such as fatal car accidents, abusive childhoods, and hostage situations. Because the aftereffects of trauma make for good drama, the list of films that portray PTSD may include some of your favorites, but it is important to keep in mind that film and other media depictions rarely reflect a real person's lived reality and instead focus on the highs and lows of a person's experience.

22. What are the psychological impacts for those who perpetrate rape, sexual assault, or dating violence?

Possible psychological impacts for those who perpetrate rape, sexual assault, or dating violence vary from person to person, of course, but there are some common reactions. Just as every person is different, so too are rapists, sexual assaulters, and those who commit dating violence. There are four categories of rapists. First, there are those people aroused by deviant sexual arousal; they become aroused by imagining violence against women, men, or people in the LGBTQIA+ community, and they commit impulsive or unplanned rapes. Second, there are people who suffer from cognitive distortions or a misunderstanding of social signals, and these people most frequently commit acquaintance rapes. Third, there are people who are motivated by anger at women, men, or people in the LGBTQIA+ community more generally, and these people are thought to be the most violent and dangerous. And fourth, there are people who are repeat offenders. They typically experienced physical or sexual abuse as a child. This sort of person is a rule breaker more generally, and committing rape is part of that pattern. In addition, we live in what is known as a rape culture, where there is an overemphasis on how women look rather than how they feel or what they think and no consideration of them as a whole human being. In addition, pornography is easily available and frequently portrays rape as a part of normal human sexuality, suggesting that the female victim is aroused by the attack rather than fearful or fighting against her attacker. All of these categories and contributing factors, however, miss the goals that rapists typically have in mind.

Some rapists attack as a form of revenge or punishment against their victims, while others punish random women, men, or people in the LGBTQIA+ community under a theory of collective liability—meaning that all women, men, or people in the LGBTQIA+ community are available to be punished or avenged for a particular person's wrongdoing. Most rapes seem to be preceded by a negative interaction with a person that the rapist considers his (most rapes are committed by men), and he held this person to a higher moralistic standard than he himself holds; domestic violence is frequently a part of that relationship too. Some rapists attack people who are the partner of a man who he perceives as having wronged them, whether they feel they are owed money, an apology, or something else; the rape of a person important to this man is seen as a way of avenging the rapist, to his distorted way of thinking. Yet others use rape as a means to prove their masculinity or to express their belief that men have the right to discipline or control others or to put them in their place. In addition, some men attack people during a burglary or robbery, as if it is an additional cruel benefit of their criminal act. In fact, some rapists believe that people who accept automobile rides home from them, people who are hitchhiking, or people at a bar have made themselves sexually available; saying no means that the victim is either teasing him or that rape is an acceptable alternative to their denial.

Some convicted rapists report to researchers that they felt powerful, near omnipotent, after their attacks. In addition, they also report that rape felt like a crime they could get away with, perhaps inadvertently acknowledging the fact that rapes are infrequently reported and even less frequently successfully prosecuted. While some rapists avoid using the word *rape* to describe their attack, this can largely be seen as a response to their shame. Psychologically, most people who rape try to rationalize why their attack was not rape at all in an attempt to keep their ego ideal of themselves intact as being a good person.

For rapists who attack people from the LGBTQIA+ community, there are similar repercussions. First, people who rape gay or queer people typically do so in a "corrective" manner; that is, they believe that raping their victim will somehow cause them to no longer be gay. In addition, people who rape LGBTQIA+ people are frequently attempting to prove their own heterosexuality, usually because of a deep-seated fear that they themselves are gay. Typically, a rapist who attacks someone who is LGBTQIA+ feels a sense of power, domination, and invincibility, as they know that rapes are so infrequently prosecuted to begin with and that LGBTQIA+ people have a harder time achieving justice in our current biased judicial system.

23. What are the legal consequences for perpetrators of rape, sexual assault, and dating violence?

Rapists who are convicted of their crime are typically found guilty of a felony and sentenced to twenty-five to thirty years' imprisonment. Most judges rely on a range of punishments and factors in determining the sentence, and the rapist may also face fines and other penalties. Judges will take into consideration aggravating and mitigating factors as they determine the length of sentence. Aggravating factors can include the rapist's criminal history or the severity of the crime, as indicated by damage to the victim's body. Mitigating factors can include acceptance of their guilt and verbal acknowledgment of the wrong done to the victim or regret or remorse expressed during the course of the trial or during the sentencing phase.

In addition, rapists are typically required to go through treatment or rehabilitation in an attempt to change their mindset and prevent future attacks. Once their sentence is served and they have been deemed no longer a threat to the community, most are required to register as a sex offender so that the public has knowledge of their crime; this frequently means that finding housing or a job is more complicated than it might be for other felons who are released after serving their time. Complicating their search for housing, some rapists and other sex offenders are not permitted to live near schools, parks, or certain neighborhoods, particularly areas where children are regularly present. They are also not permitted to own or live in a home with firearms (this is a common punishment for every person convicted of a felony). They are required to report to authorities every three years for a current photograph and must report any changes in household to the authorities. They are also required to disclose their Internet provider, screen names, and email accounts and passwords to authorities so that they may be monitored by probation officers and other law enforcement personnel. In New York, the legal code classifies rape as a Class D felony; judges can set imprisonment for a range of time, and the date of release depends on the convicted assaulter's behavior while in prison, among other considerations.

Similar to the convicted rapist, the person convicted of sexual assault faces a range of sentencing, anywhere from two to twenty years, depending on the circumstances of the assault. Every state has its own guidelines for sentencing that its judges must follow. For example, in California, the sentence can be twenty-four, thirty-six, or forty-eight months' imprisonment and potentially a $10,000 fine. Federal law instructs judges to consider factors such as the offender's criminal history and acceptance of responsibility when determining prison sentences. Federal law also sets an upper limit of twenty years' imprisonment as punishment for sexual assault.

People convicted of dating violence face either misdemeanor or felony charges, depending on the severity of the attack. If charged with misdemeanor domestic violence, the typical term for dating violence, the punishment can be up to one year in prison, plus payment of fines or restitution to the victim. In addition, a person convicted of misdemeanor domestic violence also faces potential loss of custody or visitation rights to their children and a decreased ability to find housing or employment because of their criminal record; furthermore, people convicted of domestic violence lose their right to own firearms under the Domestic Violence Offender Gun Ban. This ban also applies to those who have been served with a restraining order under domestic abuse laws. It is also illegal to give, sell, or otherwise offer a gun or other firearm to a person convicted of domestic violence.

Misdemeanor domestic violence becomes felony domestic violence if the offender caused serious bodily harm to the victim, including death, or involved other criminal conduct, such as stalking, cyberstalking, or other harassment; acts against a minor, especially very young children; violent acts or threats involving a firearm to intimidate or control the victim; or forced sexual abuse, including rape or sexual assault. People found guilty of felony domestic violence face heavier fines, sometimes several thousand dollars above what a person might face for misdemeanor domestic violence charges; imprisonment in a federal or state prison for a term greater than one year; mandatory court-ordered therapy or rehabilitation courses; and longer probation periods. In addition, a third conviction for misdemeanor domestic violence converts into a felony in many states under what is known as a three-strikes law. In addition to the harsher sentences, the person found guilty of felony domestic violence also faces loss of custody or visitation rights to their children, a decreased ability to find housing or employment, and loss of the right to own guns or other firearms and potentially a life sentence for domestic violence.

24. What are Romeo and Juliet laws?

Romeo and Juliet laws are designed to protect couples that begin dating before either of the parties turns eighteen, or to protect couples who have a small difference in age, from being found guilty of statutory rape. Statutory rape convictions in the United States carry sentences varying from one year to a life sentence, or at the extreme the death penalty, if a person is found guilty, and many states include the requirement that the convicted person register as a sex offender for the rest of their life, thus limiting housing and employment options upon release. And these sex offender registries cross state lines; that is, people required to register as a sex offender in one state also have to register in their new home state as well. These laws arose due to a perception that being labeled a sex offender for having consensual sex with a willing partner below the age of consent would be inappropriate if the couple began dating before either of them had reached the age of consent. While these laws vary from state to state and are not the law in all states, it would be beneficial to discover whether your state has a Romeo and Juliet provision in the legal code if you find yourself in this situation.

There are some common themes in the Romeo and Juliet laws in the United States. First, the minor must consent to the sexual activity; if there is no affirmative consent, it is rape. Second, the age difference should be small, between two and five years, depending on the state. Third, the person who has reached the age of consent must have a clean criminal record other than the statutory rape charge. And finally, the victim must be of a certain age for this to qualify as a Romeo and Juliet case, between ten and seventeen, depending on the state the parties live in.

It can become a significant problem when parents attempt to break up a relationship, as they may knowingly or unknowingly put one or both partners at risk of being convicted of statutory rape, sexual assault, or rape. Minors who engage in sex with another minor may find themselves accused of statutory rape, sexual assault, or rape. In heterosexual couples, the male is most frequently the only one prosecuted, even though both minors willingly participated in the sexual activity. Statutory rape, however, is a serious charge that hopes to solve a pernicious problem: every year, heterosexual male partners who are over the age of twenty causes some 50% of teen pregnancies. Laws to prevent those over the age of twenty from having sex with minors need to exist, but many jurisdictions are unclear as to where to draw that line. Some of these laws include provisions that Romeo and Juliet laws do not apply if the older person is a parent, stepparent, teacher, coach, health-care professional, or other adult with some form of authority over the minor. Some states include what they call deviant sexual behavior with a minor, a term that is not as clearly defined as it could be but appears to involve primarily oral or anal sex. These laws appear to attempt to prevent teens from participating in sexual activity that is nonreproductive in nature and likely unfairly stigmatizes gay and lesbian sexual activity.

There appear to be few provisions under Romeo and Juliet laws for couples in the LGBTQIA+ community other than those prohibiting certain sexual acts. For people from the LGBTQIA+ community along with folks who enjoy oral or anal sex, anti-sodomy laws in eight states put them at particular risk for prosecution, even though the Supreme Court struck down laws against sodomy and oral sex in 2003. Three of these eight states—Idaho, Mississippi, and South Carolina—require someone convicted under anti-sodomy laws to register as sex offenders, even if the sex they engaged in was consensual. For folks convicted in those three states, moving to another state may seem like a good idea; however, many states require people convicted in one state and required to register on the sex offender registry to also do so in their new home state. While there are appeals in process to eliminate these requirements and the double standard, before engaging in sexual activity with someone younger, it is a good idea to check the state's laws about statutory rape. See the resources section at the end of this book for more information.

Of course, the name for these laws is derived from William Shakespeare's play of the same name. In that story, two star-crossed lovers from rival families find one another, court in secrecy, marry, and spend one night together. This is one of those representations of love at first sight, as the drama takes place over a period of days rather than months or years. In Shakespeare's tragedy, both of these young lovers leave a wake of dead bodies before they eventually commit suicide. While some folks find this tale romantic and think it is a story about people who would do anything for love, more mature readings of the tale tend to find the story problematic, as Romeo initially appears onstage mourning the loss of a different love interest, Rosalind. In addition, Juliet is a mere fourteen years old and is to be married off to Paris, a local nobleman in Verona, an arranged marriage, as was the custom of the time among noble families.

25. What is the sex offender list and how does someone get on it?

The sex offender list, or registry, is a list of people who have been convicted of a sex crime at some point in their lives. These lists exist at the federal, state, and international levels and are a resource for citizens who may live near a sex offender and might change their behaviors, or the behaviors of their children, based on the sex offender's known presence in their community. In many states, the registry is known as Megan's Law and is a result of the death of Megan Kanka (in New Jersey) and her parent's activism to ensure that families would know if a sex offender moved into their neighborhood. Seven-year-old Megan was raped and killed by someone law enforcement knew as a child molester and sex offender who moved across the street from her family without their knowledge of his troubling history. In an attempt to prevent such a tragedy from occurring again, the Kankas advocated for a registry that would allow the public to search a list of known sex offenders in their neighborhoods based on postal zip codes. In other states, the registry is under the name of another person who was raped and killed by a known sex offender.

A federal list was signed into law under President George H. W. Bush on July 27, 2006, and is known as the Adam Walsh Child Protection and Safety Act. Adam Walsh was a six-year-old boy who was kidnapped from a Sears department store in Hollywood, Florida, and whose body was mutilated and dumped into local waterways. In addition to being the named child in the law, Adam is also unintentionally the cause of the "Code Adam" that some stores use to alert other employees and customers that a child is missing in an attempt to locate the child before they leave the store in the clutches of their kidnapper.

On the international level, the International Megan's Law to Prevent Child Exploitation and Other Sexual Crimes through Advance Notification of Traveling Sex Offenders seeks to prevent child sex trafficking tourism and was signed into law by President Barack Obama on February 6, 2016. It requires a unique identifier to be placed on the passports of people who are convicted of a sex act with a minor to inform people in other countries of a sex offender's past and the potential for future harm to their children. This law also requires people convicted of sex crimes to notify law enforcement prior to leaving home for international travel three weeks in advance of their trip.

People convicted of sex crimes, whether sexual assault, rape, or child sexual abuse, must register with local law enforcement within five days from their release from prison and must update their contact information every time they move and once a year if they do not move; this registration is usually a condition of parole or release from prison. In addition to these requirements, the person convicted of a sex crime must also hand over information about their Internet service provider and all of their emails and passwords so that their social media and other platforms may be monitored. If a person fails to update their contact information, they are in violation of the requirement to register and may face additional jail or prison time as a consequence. This is also indicated on the Megan's Law website.

Usually, a person must go through at least one sex offender risk assessment prior to their release from prison. Typically, risk assessment is grouped by the type of offender: first, male adult sex offenders, who are assessed pretrial and then again at release; then, juvenile sex offenders, whose information will not show up on a sex offender registry because of their age at the time of offense or release; and finally, an assessment that measures risk factors for reoffending based on things such as alcohol use or abuse, changing relationships, and stability (or instability) in housing and employment.

It should be noted that not every sex offender shows up on the list. There are reasons why a person might not have to show up on a public-facing registry, including their age at the time of offense or release; if the sex offender has no other criminal history; if the person was convicted of child pornography or sex with a minor over the age of sixteen; or if the person was convicted of sexual molestation of a child, stepchild, sibling, grandchild, or cousin but did not engage in oral copulation or penetration. In all cases, if a person scores high enough on the risk assessment, these exclusions are disregarded, and the person must register as a sex offender. Failure to register as a sex offender, if required, may result in an additional thirty years to any sentence they might receive for any new violent federal crime.

26. How can being convicted of rape or sexual assault impact someone's life?

Although fewer than 1% of rape or sexual assault cases result in a conviction, a conviction of rape or sexual assault may have lifelong repercussions.

In the near term, there is likely a prison sentence and a fine may be imposed that must be paid prior to release from prison. If a jury finds the defendant guilty, in many cases, the decision on the penalty is up to the presiding judge. Judges consider mitigating and aggravating factors in determining the sentence; mitigating factors can include a previously clean criminal history, and aggravating factors include use of a weapon, excessive violence, or a victim under the age of fifteen. Once mitigating and aggravating factors are considered, the judge may sentence the rapist or sexual assaulter to a range of two to twenty years in prison in most places across the country, although it can be up to thirty years if the rape resulted in the death of the victim, if the victim was a child, or if the victim was deemed to have been unable to provide consent due to inebriation or diminished mental capacity. While in prison, or once on probation, the convicted rapist or sexual assaulter must participate in rehabilitation exercises, the judicial system's attempt to prevent future attacks by people known to have committed rape or sexual assault in the past.

Upon release from prison, the convicted rapist or sexual assaulter must report to a parole officer and must also provide information to local law enforcement so that their information, including their photograph, shows up on the sex offender registry. In addition, there will likely be restrictions on where the convicted rapist or sexual assaulter may live or work, such as a certain number of feet away from a school, church, playground, or other places where children gather. Convicted rapists and sexual assaulters also lose their right to own firearms, and providing firearms to someone convicted of rape or sexual assault is also a criminal act for which that person may face jail time, fines, or other punishments. Finding a job is more problematic with a conviction of rape or sexual assault on one's record, as many employers view that conviction as a signal for future behaviors and want to avoid having them in their workforce, as that may make the employer legally liable if there were to be an attack against any of their employees.

People who have been convicted of rape or sexual assault may have to regularly interact with law enforcement for the rest of their lives, as they are required to report to the local law enforcement for a current photograph every one to three years; update their contact information any time there is a change, including moves to a new home, additional people living in their household, or new employment; and provide Internet service provider information along with any screen names, passwords, or other pertinent information. All of these measures were put into place to help protect the public from dangerous people; one rape or sexual assault conviction can ruin many lives, including the lives of the perpetrator, the victim, and the family members of both the perpetrator and the victim. This is particularly the case when the perpetrator and the victim are part of the same community and why stranger danger is a comforting myth that perhaps inadvertently tends to encourage us to lower our guard among those people we know and interact with regularly. The percentage of rapists or sexual assaulters who return to prison is between 20% and 35%, so these measures, while seemingly drastic or draconian, are realistic preventative measures designed to reduce the likelihood of the rapist or sexual assaulter reoffending and potentially causing a lifetime of trauma for their victims or their victims' families.

In particularly egregious cases of rape or sexual assault, in addition to the penalties outlined above, the assailant must also undergo what is known as chemical castration; this is a medical cocktail that prevents sexual arousal in cisgender males. This chemical cocktail is thought to lower sexual desire or libido and thus reduce the likelihood of pathological sexual behaviors. While chemical castration is used in an attempt to release people convicted of rape or sexual assault, folks in many neighborhoods refuse to allow these individuals in their midst, as fear for their loved ones dominates their thinking.

While the statistics on the probability of conviction for rape or sexual assault are low, they are not zero, so most people would do well to ensure that their sexual partners are enthusiastically consenting to every aspect of every sexual encounter. It is better to have an awkward moment or two during sexual activity than to face a lifetime of consequences for a few moments of harming another person.

27. How can rape and dating violence be prevented?

One of the best ways to prevent rape and dating violence is clear communication between those who are involved in relationships. For parents, it is critical that they clearly communicate about sexual behaviors and what is acceptable and what is not. Part of that conversation includes using proper names for body parts from an early age, teaching their children that some parts are to be kept to oneself (i.e., private), and assuring them that it is okay to say no to people touching them in ways that make them uncomfortable, including hugging family members at holiday gatherings or the requirement to kiss someone a child shies away from. In addition to teaching children that it is okay to trust their instincts, this also teaches children that their parents trust them to make smart choices regarding their bodies.

Parents should also teach their children that they should feel free to talk to them about secrets, as many abusers tell children to keep their actions a secret from everyone else. Parents can also teach their children that they will not get in trouble for talking about inappropriate touching or for seeing someone inappropriately touch another child. Parents can also show their children what it means to do things the right way, whether it is helping someone cross the street or ensuring that people who have dropped money get it back—modeling these types of good behaviors leads to children knowing what is right and what is wrong. Another way parents can model consensual behavior is to ask their child if they would like a hug or if they can kiss them on the cheek. The final thing parents can do is be there when their children come to them; that means putting away electronic devices, turning off the television or computer, and really listening to them, rather than doing so in an absentminded manner. Ideally, this should be part of regular parenting and not a cause for alarm for either the parent or the child. In addition, parents need to teach their children that all of their emotions are valid, even the ones that make parenting more challenging. Children who grow up in emotionally sensitive and inclusive environments appear to have an easier time avoiding sexual assault or rape as either victims or offenders.

If you are a student, there are some simple steps to ensure that rape and dating violence are not part of your experience. First, you should have a plan when you go out with your friends. Your group of friends should be people you trust, and you should all verbally agree that you will watch out for each other and leave together as a group, no matter what happens or what anyone else says. This will help ensure that no one is left in a dangerous situation. Next, if there are beverages served, be sure to keep an eye on your drink at all times and watch your friends' drinks too, if at all possible. If you are uncertain or leave your drink alone at all or without a friend nearby who can verbally tell you that no one has touched it, you should throw it out rather than guessing that it will be okay, even though that can feel like a waste of money.

In addition, know your limits with alcoholic beverages. If anyone feels extremely tired or is acting more drunk than they should be, it may be that they have been drugged by someone nearby who is waiting to do harmful things to them. If that is the case, leave the party and find professional medical help, even if there is a worry that parents, school officials, or law enforcement will find out—any of these groups of people would rather find out someone has consumed alcohol rather than learning later that they were victimized by someone unscrupulous enough to spike their drink. Feel free to lie if you need to in order to leave the party. Do not worry too much about being polite; if you are uncomfortable, trust your instincts and leave. While this is hard for a lot of people to do, as so many of us have been taught that being polite is so important, this can be a lifesaver. Many victims of rape and sexual assault report having felt threatened but did not want to overreact or appear rude to the people around them. Appear rude or as if you are overreacting: it could save you from potential trauma or a life-threatening experience.

In addition, everyone should learn to feel comfortable intervening if they see someone who appears to be at risk of rape or dating violence. Sometimes that might mean suggesting that you both leave a party when your friend, or another person you feel is vulnerable to attack, appears to be in danger; other times, it might mean stepping in between your friend, or a stranger, and their potential assailant. If you do this, you should know that there is some risk of harm to you. The person for whom you are intervening does not have to be a friend; if you see a stranger who is being threatened by someone, you could create a distraction or pretend to be the threatened person's long-lost friend so that they know they are safe with you. Be sure to ask if they know the person who appears to be harassing them and if they would like help, usually this is best done in a quiet voice so that the potential attacker cannot intervene and tell their story first. Talk to someone in authority if you are uncomfortable intervening or putting yourself between the victim and the attacker; contact the person in charge, the security guard, a bartender, or some other person who works there or call the police if you feel that it is necessary. You might feel more comfortable enlisting others to help you intervene for someone. It also helps intimidate the attacker if there are a lot of people intervening. Some folks have intervened as a group and stopped some pretty bad things from happening to another person.

Another way to help ensure that everyone stays safe is to advocate for rape and dating violence prevention programs in your school, church youth group, after-school program, or other places in your community, if they do not already have one. You can also rate your school's sexual assault prevention program using RAINN's Navigator tool (available in the resources section of this book). RAINN also offers numerous training materials that students or other people may use in conjunction with their school's sexual assault prevention program. Spread the word about sexual assault prevention programs through your social media network, whether that is on your Instagram feed, TikTok videos, or other social media outlets; talk about what constitutes consent with your friends and your partner (this especially could make a great TikTok video); and join your campus's *Vagina Monologues* or SlutWalk. If activities like these do not exist at your school, find out how to start one. Get started by checking out the resources at the end of this book.

28. Is there anything individuals can do to help minimize their chances of becoming a victim of rape or dating violence?

Yes! Foremost, *always* listen to your instincts. When you feel that there is a dangerous person or situation, leave immediately, even if you are worried that you might be seen as rude. It is better to be rude than to be sexually assaulted or worse. Stay aware of your surroundings and avoid going alone to areas you perceive as dangerous (whether based on instinct or news reports of crime in the area). Walk with your head up, confidently and at a steady pace, and make direct eye contact with others on the street. Do not use music headphones when walking alone or wear without sound or with the sound on very low volume. A lot of people make themselves inadvertent potential victims by not being as aware as they could be when out in public. Be sure to keep your cell phone charged before leaving home and take it with you. Avoid going out alone with someone you do not know well. Tell friends or family where you are going when you leave, and if they are not present when you leave, text them or leave a note so they know where to find you. If plans change while you are out, be sure to let someone you trust know where you are going, with whom, and when you expect to return home. If you feel you are in imminent danger, run from the situation rather than waiting to find out for certain that it is unsafe. If you are afraid that you are being followed, go directly to the nearest open public space with lots of people and bright lights, perhaps a grocery store, gas station, or other facility where there are a lot of people around.

When you go out to parties, go with a group of friends who promise to look out for one another. Have a plan—everyone goes together and everyone leaves together is a pretty good policy. Have friends watch your beverage when you are away from it and do the same for them. Date rape drugs are odorless and tasteless; if your beverage is spiked with one of these drugs, there is no way to know before drinking it. Never accept beverages from a stranger or one that you did not watch being poured. Stay alert and aware of where the exits are located. If you are in a crowded room and need to leave a friend for a moment for a bathroom break, let them know where you are going and when you expect to be back or go together. Look behind you to let anyone following know that you see them.

Avoid posting too much personal information on social media, especially social media that uses GPS to tell friends where you are located. Perhaps turn that function off on your cell phone for nights out, especially if you know that an ex-partner would like to follow you or surprise you while you are out; this can help prevent their ability to stalk you in real life. In the past, people thought that persistence meant true love, but all of that has changed. Now we know that these behaviors are not a sign of true love but rather of obsession or a refusal to respect the wishes and boundaries of a former significant other. If you jog or run outdoors for exercise, try to vary your route and the time when you run so that predators cannot plan for your arrival at a specific place and time. If your school offers self-defense classes, take them. If your school does not offer self-defense classes, ask them to. If need be, start a petition to bring self-defense classes to your campus. Add your school's police department to your contact list so that you can dial it in a hurry if necessary. If your school has emergency call boxes and you feel threatened, use the call box to call campus police. If your school does not have emergency call boxes, ask for them and start a petition drive or ask your student government to organize a student-led campaign to make it happen.

If you see a stranger who is in danger of sexual assault or dating violence, ask them if they are safe and, if need be, help them escape the dangerous situation. If you have experienced dating violence and have broken up with that partner, be alert to their coming back into your life by suddenly becoming friends with your friends on social media or by stalking you in person or on social media. It may become necessary to file for a restraining order to keep them away from you, which is usually pretty easily done at a local police station; see the resources section of this book for helpful guidance. Stalking a former partner is serious business. It is not a sign of love or devotion; rather, it is a refusal to admit that the relationship is over as well as a manifestation of obsession and a desire to control the other person. See the resources on stalking at the end of this book.

Suggest these same tips to friends and family members who might need to know how to take precautions to ensure their own safety or so that they can help you stay safe from dating violence.

29. Is it possible to completely eliminate rape and dating violence in the future?

Yes! Unfortunately, it begins with how we raise our children, so this is a long-term project that all of us need to work on together. When we become parents (if we choose to become parents, that is), we have to be much clearer about consent: what it is, what it is not, and how to ask for it. We have to be much more comfortable talking about sex and sexuality with our own parents, partners, and children and how to handle it when a partner does not consent or changes their mind in the middle of a sex act. We also need to let our kids tell us when they do not want to hug a relative and respect their desires too. That means that when someone else's child does not want to hug or kiss us, we have to be all right with that and respect their bodily autonomy and ability to say no to unwanted touching. Autonomy, or the lack of autonomy, over our bodies is the first way that a lot of us learn about consent.

Next, we have to call out rape culture when we see it, whether it is an off-color joke, an advertisement, a friend catcalling people in the street or at a club, or a friend groping women at a club. Rape culture suggests that women in particular are here for men to look at and that women should appreciate their interest in them sexually. If you see sexism in video games, movies, or television programming, contact the producer and complain. Use the Bechdel test to see whether films represent multi-dimensional female characters; see the reference at the end of this book for information about the Bechdel test.

In addition, we also have to call out toxic masculinity and stereotypes about men that end up hurting them and the people around them. Male desire is not something that requires gratification from anyone—ever. Actions and words that define masculinity as only strength and stoicism are harmful, especially when they are at the expense of seeing men as compassionate and caring—the emotional equivalent of anyone else. This includes the sexual double standard that numerous partners for men is laudatory, but numerous partners for women makes them damaged goods. It also means that when someone tells us they have been sexually assaulted or raped or are a victim of dating or domestic violence that we believe them rather than question what they did to deserve that sort of treatment. It is also critical that we call rape what it is and avoid euphemisms such as "nonconsensual sex," "sexual misconduct," or "unwanted sex." Rape is rape, and euphemisms like these do more harm than good.

We also have to become much more comfortable with intervening when we see something inappropriate happening. While this may include an element of danger, it is critical that people who might commit violent acts know that it is no longer socially acceptable. Whether it is a friend, teammate, or family member, we should let them know that we will not tolerate that sort of behavior and will intervene if they cross that line.

This is especially important for men to do with other men, as cisgender men are typically the aggressors in these sorts of situations.

Finally, we have to advocate for programs at work and in schools that support people coming forward with their stories. All too often, victims of sexual assault, dating violence, or rape are hesitant to tell their stories because of fear or shame. Some survivors fear telling their stories because they are afraid of being fired from the job, for example. Some victims are ashamed of their victimization, as if they were part of the reason it happened. This is another facet of our rape culture—victims feeling shame rather than rapists. The repercussions for rape should always fall on the shoulders of the aggressor, not the victim. We should also support organizations that seek to help survivors of sexual assault, rape, and dating violence.

❖❖❖

Seeking Help

30. What services are available for victims of rape and sexual assault?

Services for victims of rape or sexual assault vary from city to city, campus to campus, and state to state. But there are some national organizations that can help point you in the right direction. First, there is the National Sexual Assault Hotline, 1-800-656-4673; this line is staffed twenty-four hours a day, every day of the year, and provides information for rape and sexual assault victims, their supporters, and allies about resources in their area. In addition, the Rape, Abuse, and Incest National Network (RAINN) provides information online; the information is categorized, and a chat window is available if you are unsure where to look for your exact situation. Be sure to look at the resources at the end of this book for more information about these organizations.

An Abuse, Rape, Domestic Violence Aid and Resource Center (AARDVARC) provides resources for sexual abuse, rape, and domestic violence survivors and their allies, and it provides programs for victims. This group was started and is run by survivors, and the topics covered are those chosen by survivors, including: stalking, sexual assault and rape, hate crimes, harassment, domestic violence, cyberbullying, and antisocial behavior. The After Silence page provides a forum where survivors can talk to one another, find resources in their area, and view blog posts where people work through their trauma, offer support to one another, and post poetry reflecting their experiences.

The End the Silence campaign is a group of websites that focus locally on sharing poetry, art, and stories to support victims of sexual violence; the sites also provide links to RAINN and the National Sexual Assault Hotline as well as links to some of the more prolific poets contributing to the site. Similarly, Fort Refuge is a survivor-to-survivor network that provides peer support through online chats to anyone over the age of sixteen. It also offers a library of resources, including articles about rape and sexual assault, domestic violence, religious violence, PTSD, and anxiety and seventy-eight full-length documentaries on a wide range of topics related to rape, sexual assault, and domestic violence. Pandora's Project also offers peer-to-peer support for victims of sexual assault, rape, and sexual abuse worldwide as well as articles for survivors and their allies, including resources for legal action, recovery, and volunteering and activism— something many survivors find gratifying and healing. Survivor's Chat is exactly that, a place where survivors can talk to one another about the trauma of rape, sexual assault, or sexual abuse, whether it happened when they were children or as adults; it also provides resources for people who have recently experienced trauma, including international phone numbers for suicide prevention lines, phone numbers for sexual assault hotlines, links to other survivor websites and the sex offender registry, advice on coping skills and healing from trauma, and articles on eating disorders, dissociative identity disorder, and self-harm.

Different from those listed above, 7 Cups of Tea offers peer-to-peer support and professional therapy for $150 per month; there are over 180 professional therapists and over 300,000 specially trained listeners. This site has so far helped over twenty-five million people. It also offers articles on self-worth and how to develop it and information about eye movement desensitization and reprocessing therapy (EMDR), addiction, anxiety, depression, domestic violence, loneliness, mindfulness, PTSD, self-affirmations, self-harm, and therapy.

The Trevor Project provides support via online chat for LGBTQIA+ people who have experienced sexual assault or rape that is confidential and secure and also welcomes younger LGBTQIA+ folks, ages thirteen to twenty-four years old, and those who are exploring their sexuality and want to know more. The Trevor Project is named for the 1994 short film project *Trevor*, which focuses on a young man who realizes he is homosexual and faces backlash from the people around him. See the resources guide at the end of this book for a link to the film. In addition, the local United Way can often provide resources that are location specific through its 211 program: simply dial 211 from your location, and you will be connected to a representative who can direct you to those local resources.

It is important to note that while the availability of services differs drastically based on one's location, historically speaking, there were *no* services for victims of rape or sexual assault in the past. Instead, all people who were sexually assaulted or raped were taught, either explicitly or implicitly, that silence was their best bet. If a person had been sexually assaulted or raped, most of the time, they kept that to themselves and tried to get over the shame and guilt that they felt, without access to psychological help, communities of care, or other resources. This means that a lot of older people who had these experiences still carry that with them, as they have likely not sought psychological counseling for their victimization. This can also be a reason why some older folks are unwilling to listen when people talk about their own victimization; while it is hurtful to be rejected by someone we respect, it is helpful to remember that we have resources now that they did not have when they were younger.

31. What services are available for victims of dating violence?

Similar to rape victims, there are numerous services for people who have experienced dating violence. There is a list of the following services in the resources section of this book. A good place to start would be the Love Is Respect website, which offers support via chat or phone twenty-four hours a day, seven days a week. In addition to helping people in crisis, this site offers a plethora of healthy relationship advice, including a dating FAQ sheet, advice on how to develop healthy relationships and what to look for in a partner, and guidance about breakups. There is also information for people who abuse their partners and people who support friends who are experiencing dating violence and information about dating violence in the LGBTQIA+ community, what constitutes dating violence through quizzes, and other materials to help a person experiencing dating violence negotiate their way out of the trauma.

The National Center for Victims of Crime offers a section on dating violence focused specifically on teens in addition to numerous other options for people who have experienced an assault of any other kind. The bulletins for teens focus on dating violence, define the terms related to dating violence, offer guidance on what to do if you are a victim of dating violence, and tell folks how to get help, either for themselves or for a friend. In addition, there are links to national hotlines for victims of violence, including the National Teen Dating Violence Hotline. While this site does not offer support per se, it can help people figure out whether their experience is dating violence and can help people find the resources they need.

In addition, the Victim Legal Network of DC offers assistance to folks in the Washington, DC, area who are experiencing dating or domestic violence, along with many other sorts of victimizations. It offers services for people who are more broadly speaking victims of crimes, including dating and domestic violence, and advice for how to get help in that area. In addition to calling the police, or as an alternative to the police, it also offers help that is not connected to law enforcement. For victims of sexual assault or rape, there is information on where to get a medical examination and how to obtain a protective order against an abuser; it also conveniently lists hospitals in the area. It also suggests that folks who are in a relationship that has become abusive use private browser windows (on Google Chrome, this window is called incognito) so the abuser cannot track the victim's search history for help in determining whether they are trying to escape the toxic relationship. Notably, the site provides assistance for victims of crime in seven different languages; while this site may not be suitable for everyone across the country, it does provide a model of what such a service might look like in other communities.

DAWN provides assistance to people in the deaf community and promotes healthy relationships through resource referrals to medical and legal professionals, case management, peer advocacy, counseling, support groups, resiliency education, restorative justice, and nontraditional healing services. It also collaborates with cultural organizations and associations. This organization is based in Washington, DC, and provides services to deaf people in that area.

The National Indigenous Women's Resource Center offers access to resources specifically geared toward Indigenous women. This organization offers culturally sensitive confidential support and referrals to local resources through the StrongHearts Native Helpline. This helpline is available from 7:00 a.m. to 10:00 p.m. (CST). This group is affiliated with numerous organizations, including the Indian Law Resource Center, Mending the Sacred Hoop (focused on southwestern Indigenous women), the National Congress of American Indians, and the Tribal Law and Policy Institute. They also have resources specifically geared toward Indigenous teens and young adults to help them form healthy relationships and a section on dating violence within this community.

LAMBDA Legal provides support for people in the LGBTQIA+ community through its Anti-Violence Project (AVP). The AVP provides assistance for people who have been victims of hate crimes, dating and domestic violence, harassment, discrimination, police misconduct and abuse, and prisoner neglect, assault, and abuse through peer-to-peer counseling, a twenty-four-hour bilingual hotline (English and Spanish), and advocacy and accompaniment to police, courts, and other service providers. It advises that you call 911 if you are experiencing an emergency at that moment or to call or email the organization or contact the National Domestic Violence Hotline.

Similar to LAMBDA Legal, Trans Lifeline provides support for trans people, through peer-to-peer counseling. This nonprofit lifeline provides support for trans people and those who are questioning their sexual identities. It can provide both emotional and financial aid to those in the trans and questioning communities in emergency situations. This Lifeline was founded in 2014 and remains the only hotline staffed entirely by trans people. In addition, there are opportunities for trans people to receive training to field calls to the hotline—a position that is paid for operators and team leads. This in itself can prove lifesaving for trans folks, as unemployment is an experience that many trans folks face. In addition, the Trans Lifeline also offers microgrants to trans people who find themselves economically disadvantaged.

In addition, the Women's Law Project focuses on people experiencing dating or domestic violence and provides information in three categories: legal information, abuse information, and places that can help. What distinguishes this site from many others is that categories of advice for legal information and places that can help has a drop-down menu so that you can choose your state and get specific information that will help you make your next move. For example, the categories for help for people in California include advocates and shelters, finding a lawyer, courthouse locations, and sheriff's departments. Many of their pages are bilingual, Spanish and English, with more being added regularly. There is additional information for people who are immigrants and for people who are either in the military or whose abuser is in the military.

The National Domestic Violence Hotline offers advice for people in dating or domestically violent relationships, including creating a safety plan, support for victims and their family members, information about why people stay in abusive relationships, legal services, assistance for deaf people, advice about pets and domestic violence, what to expect when you contact the hotline, and tech advice to ensure your safety. In addition, there is a respective section on LGBTQIA+, immigrants, disabled people, and pregnancy and dating or domestic violence. They also provide a plethora of information about forming healthy relationships, how to set boundaries, creating healthy communication, trust, equality, and consent in relationships.

The National Resource Center on Domestic Violence is a one-stop shop for a variety of resources for victims of dating or domestic violence. It advises to call 911 or call the National Domestic Violence Hotline if you are in immediate danger. In addition, there are links to culturally specific resources, including the Asian Pacific Islander Institute on Gender-Based Violence (API-GBV) and Casa de Esperanza: National Latin@ Network of Healthy Families and Communities.

The API-GBV provides information about domestic and dating violence against women of Asian American and Pacific Islander (AAPI) heritage, focusing on abusive international marriages, dating abuse and sexual assault for teens and young adults, domestic violence, elder abuse, forced marriage, HIV and intimate partner violence, homicide and domestic violence, LGBTQIA+ violence, sexual violence, and human trafficking. In addition, it also serves as an advocate for people in the AAPI community, providing information about child custody in domestically violent relationships, advocacy for Muslim women and Pacific Islanders, and a U.S.-based directory of domestic and gendered violence programs serving the AAPI community.

Casa de Esperanza: National Latin@ Network of Healthy Families and Communities features a twenty-four-hour hotline and focuses its efforts on culturally relevant research to inform the creation of new strategies to engage Latinas and their communities to end domestic violence, and a public policy initiative based in Washington, DC, that brings the Latinx experience to legislators by translating policy decisions into the real repercussions for this community. It also provides training for Latin@ and domestic violence organizations as well as mainstream organizations that serve the Latinx community. The website offers help figuring out whether what you are experiencing is domestic or dating violence, considerations for children (if any), who you should talk to, immigrants' rights, and support for friends helping friends in abusive relationships. While this organization is based in St. Paul, Minnesota, it is the largest organization focused on ending domestic violence in Latinx households nationwide. The organization also provides training materials for activists throughout Latin America and the United States.

Ujima: The National Center on Violence against Women in the Black Community focuses on helping Black women find resources in dating or domestically violent relationships. They are working on putting together a national list of resources but offer a hotline in the meantime. This organization offers definitions of dating and domestic violence, sexual violence, and community violence.

The organization Live Your Dreams offers numerous resources, including warning signs of domestic violence; a general overview of sexual assault and abuse; how to create a safety plan; how to find a local domestic violence shelter; information about custody issues; financial tips for survivors, including how to rebuild your finances; how to find low-cost or free legal advice; and what to say when someone you know is being abused.

The U.S. Office of Health and Human Service's Office on Women's Services offers resources by state on violence against women that help people determine whether their experience was dating or domestic violence as well as information on sexual assault and rape, other types of violence against women, and the effects of violence against women, and it has resources for allies of victims of dating or domestic violence.

32. What should I do or not do immediately following a rape?

If you have been raped or think you may have been raped, the first thing to do is to remind yourself that it is not your fault. Nothing you did or said could have caused or prevented your assault. In fact, the only thing that causes rape is rapists. Next, ensure that you are in a safe place and not subject to further assault. If you are not in a safe place, either call a friend to come to you or leave the place where you feel endangered. If your attacker was someone you know—or thought you knew—you should know that up to 70% of all sexual assaults and rapes are committed by someone the victim knows; that means there is no use in beating yourself up for what happened because of the stranger danger myth.

Once safe, it is important that you do nothing to change the way you look: do not shower immediately afterward, even though you really want to; do not change clothes; and do not wash your hands or hair. If you decide later on that you want to report your rape to law enforcement, it is important to have had medical professionals collect evidence that was present on your body to help strengthen your case. Either way, you should seek medical care for several reasons. First, you may have injuries that need to be treated, and some of these injuries may be internal and therefore not visible to you or others without medical equipment. Second, you should be tested for sexually transmitted diseases so that you can receive treatment; there are medications available if you think you may have been exposed to HIV or other sexually transmitted diseases. You may decide that you want to use emergency contraception, and that is best taken within five days of the rape.

When you go for medical care, you should know that you do not have to relive every moment of your assault; in fact, nearly all medical professionals will only ask you two questions: did your assailant use a condom, and what orifices were penetrated. You might want to bring a friend with you so that you have a familiar face nearby while you go through the examination or have someone to talk to on the way there or on the way back, as these experiences—the rape and the medical examination—are likely traumatic.

Next, you should likely reach out to someone you trust, whether it is a friend or family member, to talk about your experience. If you feel that you cannot talk to friends or family, you will also find support through a local therapist or a state or national hotline. Perhaps the hardest part about recovery from rape is the emotional aftermath. Group therapy along with individual counseling can help, as can journaling, walking, and meditation. If you are experiencing unusual anxiety, consider it an aftereffect of your assault and work toward calming yourself through mindful breathing exercises or by reminding yourself that you are not currently in danger. Therapy may be useful to help you recall your assault in a supportive environment so you can process the experience and find peace from within.

Remember that there is no timeline on processing your experience. Sometimes memories may pop up unexpectedly quite some time after the assault. Some people who have been raped experience PTSD as a result, so it is important to get help to emotionally process the event. Getting psychological help does not guarantee you will not have PTSD, but it will likely reduce the intensity or the duration of it.

One of the most important things to do after rape is to be patient with yourself and work to ensure that you take care of yourself, physically, emotionally, and mentally. Avoid staying home out of fear or because you are worried about what other people might think. Rape is far more common in our culture than you might imagine, and most people are empathetic rather than judgmental. If you find that people are judgmental, feel free to walk away from the conversation. If you are unsure of where to get help, your local Planned Parenthood might be a good place to start. Remember, there is no timeline on when you should be over something like rape. If you are still traumatized months or years later, that is fine and does not indicate that you are doing anything wrong.

33. I think I may have been raped, but I'm not sure. What should I do?

The guidelines for what to do if you think you have been raped are strikingly similar to the advice for people who know they have been raped. First, you should know that what may have happened to you is not your fault; there is nothing you could have done or not done to prevent the assault. The blame goes to the person who attacked you, or forced you to have sex despite your saying no, or had sex with you when you were too high or inebriated to say no. Then, be sure that you are safe and not in any danger of being attacked again. If you do not feel safe, either leave the place or call a friend to come to you. If you think you have been raped, it is equally important that you seek medical care as soon as possible, regardless of whether you choose to prosecute your assailant or report your rape to the police. The medical professional will not ask you awkward questions about what you were wearing or whether you had alcohol; most are only going to ask whether your assailant used a condom and what orifices were penetrated. Seeking medical attention also has the benefit of ensuring that you receive Plan B, an emergency contraceptive, if you are not on any other form of birth control, and medications for STDs, including HIV, if you think you may have been exposed. It is also important for a medical professional to retrieve biological materials from your body in case you do decide that what happened was rape and decide to prosecute your assailant by contacting law enforcement. In addition, many of the injuries from rape are invisible to most people because they are frequently internal. Seeking medical help immediately can help reduce complications from these injuries.

Many people who think they have been raped find comfort in group therapy and individual psychological counseling sessions. Group therapy helps by providing a supportive environment for you to process what happened to you and helps you feel less alone. Group therapy typically operates by all members agreeing to strict confidentiality and creating an environment where people feel safe sharing what was likely the scariest experience of their lives. Hearing other people's stories helps you to learn that you truly did not deserve what happened to you, as we can often see other people more clearly than we can see ourselves. Most people who are raped know the person that attacked them, and up to 70% of all rapes occur between people who know one another; so it is no use blaming yourself or dwelling on what-if scenarios. You also might find support from a close friend or family member, if you feel comfortable sharing your experience with them.

The hardest part of sexual assault and rape is processing the emotional aftermath. It is challenging to begin to trust other people again, especially in our more intimate relationships, as they are the most likely ones to trigger those traumatic memories. Your intimate partner may need to know what has happened to you and should support you in a loving way to help you overcome hesitancy or resistance to intimacy. You should explain why touching you in that particular area is triggering your memory of the attack so that your partner can avoid that during foreplay or coitus. Your partner's patience will be essential to your sexual healing and ability to enjoy intimacy again, as will your own patience. There is no timeline on healing from sexual assault, and every person progresses and experiences these intrusive memories unexpectedly. Many people who think they were raped find that they experience PTSD, with flashbacks, dreams, and intrusive thoughts that interrupt their daily activities. Therapy can help those who experience PTSD; see elsewhere in this book for more information about this complication of rape.

It is important for your healing that you continue to do much of what you did prior to your rape. Avoid staying home out of fear; no one will judge you, and you are likely to find that other people are empathic if you choose to talk about your experience. Be patient with yourself and trust your instincts. Seek help from a mental health professional if you are experiencing anxiety, a new desire to isolate socially, or other aftereffects that you do not think you can handle on your own. There is certainly no shame in asking for help from a mental health professional, even if you come from a community that typically frowns on such interventions. In addition, a mental health professional will not share that you are seeing them, if you do decide to go; this protection is afforded to us through the Health Insurance Portability and Accountability Act, otherwise known as HIPAA.

If you are unsure of where to start to find a therapist or counselor, your local Planned Parenthood might be a good place to start, as might your own trusted medical professional. You should also know that medical professionals, such as doctors, nurses, and other medical personnel, are prohibited from talking about someone's access to medical care to someone else, such as a parent or guardian, without your express permission. You will have the choice to make your information available to other people or to keep it entirely private when you check into a doctor's office, hospital, or other medical facility. There is typically a one-page document that you will be asked to sign that has a place to put the names of folks you want to have access to your medical information. That means that unless you want them to, no one else will know you have been to seek medical care for a potential rape or for any other medical need.

34. I think I may have crossed a line during sex and am worried that what I did could be considered rape. What should I do?

First, if you think you crossed a line or that your partner decided to not have sex while you were in the middle of copulation, then you probably did cross that line. The truth is that around two-thirds of rapes and 73% of sexual assaults happen between people who already know one another. If you think you have crossed a line, it is likely you raped someone you know and perhaps someone you care about. There is no way to undo what has been done, but you might consider apologizing to the person you raped. While this will not help you if they decide to file rape charges, it will help them as they work to recover from the trauma you inflicted. It shows that you take ownership of your actions, no matter how terrible and shameful, and also allows for the opportunity to begin processing the fact that you made an intimate act into one of violence; that is, if you can admit it, you can begin on your own path toward self-forgiveness. If you offer your victim a truly mature apology rather than an "I'm sorry if you feel that way" apology, then you can begin to change the behaviors that allowed you to do that. Of course, this advice comes with a caveat or warning that if your victim has said that they never want to hear from or see you again, it is your job to respect those boundaries. Crossing boundaries is what caused you to violate the trust of someone that you likely care about. You might find the following useful as an exercise to help you work toward regaining your self-respect and self-esteem.

A mature apology has a minimum of three components. The first component is an acknowledgment of what you have done. This should be pretty detailed and specific. Something along the lines of, "I'm sorry that I continued to touch you after you said no," would be a good start. There should be no "kind of" or "sort of" involved in this part. It should be a simple declarative statement of what happened. The second component is an acknowledgment of the harm you have done to the victim. Depending on your relationship to the victim, this could be something like, "I imagine you're pretty mad at me and hurt that I could do that to you" or "I understand that you're probably really upset with me right now." And the third and final component is a promise to never behave in that way again. This should include specifics, such as, "I'll never drink again and make out with somebody" or "I'll never _____ and _____," filling in the blanks with whatever it is that you did. Again, no "sort of" or "kind of" is allowed here either.

If you really want to show your victim that you support them, you could offer to take them to a medical facility to ensure that there are no injuries. Be aware that many folks will not want to accept your offer, but offering demonstrates that you care about the health and well-being of the person you injured.

You should know that nearly half of all sexual assaults and rapes occur when alcohol is involved. Alcohol is a drug that tends to dampen the conscience and therefore encourages people to do things they might otherwise not do. That does not mean it is the alcohol's fault; rather, our decreased inhibitions allow us to cross boundaries we normally would not. Alcohol also increases our expectations of sexual activity or causes us to think that our victim wants sexual activity when they do not or that they are sexually available when they are just consuming alcohol with no intention of having sex, either specifically with you or with anyone at all. Avoiding alcohol in the future might prevent a repeat of this hopefully onetime mistake.

35. I think I've committed dating violence. What should I do?

First, you should know that dating violence is not about getting mad at your partner; rather, it is about power and control. Even if you feel as though your anger is caused by your partner and whatever it is that they were doing (or not doing), it is never about whatever that is. Couples fight about some pretty strange things, and in an abusive relationship, those topics can frequently trigger feelings of rage or a sense of being disrespected. People who feel that they are losing control tend to lash out at their partners, especially if they fear that their partner might leave them or they are worried that their partner will find someone new who will treat them better.

You should also know that people who witness violence in their home between their parents or between a parent and their partner are more likely to engage in domestically violent activity themselves in dating relationships or once they settle down with one partner and live with them. That means that if you watched one or more parent engage in violent activity in the home, you are more likely to engage in similar behavior, despite your strongest feelings that it was not right when you were younger. The trouble is that these domestically violent relationships fail to teach children how adults deal with frustration or anger at their intimate partner, and that leads to a sense that being violent is acceptable and perhaps comfortable in a really weird way.

Another reason witnessing this behavior is problematic is that it fails to teach how to express your needs and desires in a way that other people can hear and respond to in a positive manner. It may be that couples therapy would help to resolve your conflicts with your partner and help you either achieve a mature, mutually beneficial relationship with one another or set you up for successful relationships with other people in the future. In addition, if you tend to be an aggressive person, it is likely that you will end up in combative relationships with other aggressive people at work or at home. One sign of being abusive or aggressive might include frequent job changes, which you feel were not your fault, or claims that the boss just "didn't like" you or always had it in for you.

There are serious consequences for dating and domestic violence. Even if your partner does not file charges against you, you are unlikely to experience empathy for your partner and their point of view on important topics. This means that while you may have sexual relations with someone, you are unlikely to achieve true intimacy with them. In addition, if your partner does file charges against you and you are found guilty, in addition to jail time, you also face fines and may be reported to the Domestic Violence Database. This is similar to the sex offender registry and is used as a tool to prevent partners in the future from being abused by you. You will also lose your Second Amendment rights to own firearms: if you acquire weapons through some loophole or are found to have firearms in your possession, you may face additional jail time, as it is frequently a violation of the terms of probation, or other penalties. This is true whether you are found guilty of misdemeanor or felony domestic violence. This is also true of people who work in law enforcement or the military; that is, there is no exception for law enforcement officials or military personnel to the provision depriving them of access to firearms. If you had intended to become a police officer or to join the military and are convicted of dating or domestic violence, you will not be allowed to carry a handgun or other firearm and will be unable to fulfill your dream of becoming a police officer or following your military career path.

36. I am in a sexual relationship with someone older or younger than me and am worried about accusations of statutory rape. What should I do?

An age difference of a couple of years in either direction is usually not a problem, but it can be if there is a significant age difference or if the person you are dating is above or below a certain age, depending on what state you and your partner live in. One of the reasons this is a problem is because of the laws designed to protect children from being victimized by people looking to exploit them for sexual purposes. There are other dynamics at work here as well; for example, there may be a difference in power expectations or the level of sexual maturity of the younger person. If you are dating someone several years older, they may have expectations for a dating experience that is drastically different from your own. For example, they may want to progress in the relationship faster than you do. For many of us, our beginning relationships moved slowly past holding hands to cuddling or kissing the other person. Part of healthy sexual activity is being allowed to work out for oneself what one likes and does not like in a supportive environment. If you are dating someone much older, their expectations may guide your sexual development in ways that you might not want to explore or at a pace that makes you uncomfortable. In addition, it may be the case that your partner is above the age that is legally allowed to sexually interact with someone under the age of eighteen. It is best to check your local laws regarding sex with a minor before proceeding any further with a new relationship with someone older, as the consequences for them may include imprisonment, fines, and a lifetime on the sex offender registry—and that frequently includes a lifetime of job and housing limitations.

If you are an older person dating a minor, you should know the laws in your state regarding statutory rape and perhaps Romeo and Juliet laws, if those exist where you live. Check out question 24 about Romeo and Juliet laws and the resources section in this book so you have a basic understanding of how these laws work. There are some legal complications involved in dating a minor, including the very real possibility that you could be arrested, found guilty of statutory rape (regardless of what your partner says in terms of consenting to sexual activity), imprisoned, fined, and forced to register as a sex offender for the rest of your life. Furthermore, even if your partner consents to sexual activity or if you did not know the person was under eighteen, you are still criminally liable. That is, your ignorance of the person's real age does not protect you. Federal law prohibits anyone over the age of eighteen from engaging in sexual activity with someone aged twelve to sixteen if there is greater than four years' difference in age between them. Most states set their own age of consent, and it can vary from as young as ten years old to sixteen years old.

In addition to the possible legal consequences, there are other considerations, including your partner's emotional maturity and experience with sexual activity. If you plan to continue the relationship with your partner, you should both acknowledge the age difference and think about the long-term consequences of dating and potentially solidifying that relationship either through marriage or moving in together. The other thing to keep in mind is that you and your partner will change through the years; you will want to do some sort of check-in together for the rest of the relationship to ensure that you are both on the same page emotionally and sexually.

You will also want to have an action plan for when people criticize you and your partner for having chosen each other despite the age difference; you will want to know ahead of time what your partner's or your response might be. Finally, know that the potential for legal jeopardy does have an end, such as when your partner turns eighteen, or if the relationship were to end otherwise.

37. If I seek medical help or counseling for rape or dating violence, do I have to report the incident to the police? Are those helping me required to report the incident to the police?

If you seek medical help for rape or domestic violence, you do not have to report the incident to the police. However, medical professionals may be required to report your case to the police. In most states, health-care professionals are required to report dating and domestic violence to the police, but the information required varies from state to state. This practice is known as mandated reporters and can include people such as your teachers, social workers, or other people with whom you interact who may come to know of your rape or dating violence experience. On the other hand, few states mandate reporting rape to law enforcement officials, but most states require reporting injuries that are consistent with rape. Most states require the patient's name, a description of the patient's injuries, and the name or identity of the perpetrator, if known. While these are the minimums required by law, the report may go into greater detail than that, depending on the individual health-care professional you encounter, the current practices at that particular facility, and what is required by that particular state. Federal law requires that the health-care provider tell the patient that a mandatory report must be submitted except in cases where reporting would put the patient at greater risk for retaliation by their attacker. Intimate partner violence is against the law in every state, and this reporting is required of health-care providers. Health-care professionals are required to report verbally as soon as possible with follow-up written reports due within two days.

Best practices in these cases require that health-care providers tell patients about their reporting responsibility prior to any examination or consultation so that the patient may make an informed decision about what to tell. Not telling their patients about their responsibility to report is another way that people in the health-care system have failed victims of dating and domestic violence and rape in the past; the disclosure at the beginning of the encounter ensures that the patient knows that their rights are protected.

You should know that this responsibility to report is not viewed as being a 100% positive thing. Many health-care providers view the reporting responsibility as taking autonomy away from a person who has already been victimized as problematic and that this may prevent their patients from returning for care, especially in an emergency situation. In addition, reporting may provoke further attacks if law enforcement shows up to the partner's house or place of employment (in cases of dating or domestic violence or intimate partner violence). Reporting may also cause the patient to avoid future health care if they are afraid that their attack will be reported to police and their partner will face legal consequences; this is especially true if they are also financially dependent on their partner or if they know that this will provoke another attack from their partner. Several states have revised their laws so that health-care providers must refer their patients who have been victims of dating or domestic violence or rape to domestic violence programs or other victim services agencies in an attempt to protect the patient from further victimization or other harm. If you are in doubt about seeking medical care, please refer to the resources section of this book.

While health-care providers are required to report dating and domestic violence and rape, it is unclear what happens afterward. Does law enforcement necessarily become involved? Is the patient's future safety ensured? Ideally, medical professionals will coordinate care with outside agencies that help people who have been victims of dating or domestic violence or rape to ensure the patient's well-being and future action plan for returning to full health and well-being. In addition, reporting an attack to local law enforcement may help expedite restraining orders and ensure that the attacker is brought to justice swiftly.

38. Should I get a restraining order? How do I get one?

Sometimes a person's experience with another person is terrible or threatening enough to require law enforcement to help maintain distance from that person. This can happen through dating or domestic violence, sexual harassment, assault, rape, or stalking. If you believe that someone you know is intent on causing harm to you or people you care about, you may want to consider getting a restraining order. Typically, you can find information about restraining orders by simply searching the Internet for your state or county. In California, for example, there are two types of restraining orders: a civil harassment restraining order and a domestic violence restraining order for people who have been in a relationship with the person who is now harassing or threatening harm to them.

Restraining orders require approval from a court official, typically a judge. You will want to have all of your forms ready, including a notice to law enforcement outlining who you are, who you have filed a restraining order against, where they live and work, and whether they have access to weapons, such as guns. If you are staying someplace that your attacker does not know about, leave that address or that person's information off the paperwork you file with the court, as it becomes public record and therefore becomes accessible to the person you are trying to avoid. In many jurisdictions, courts have a self-help center where knowledgeable people will review your paperwork before you file for your restraining order. Once you have your forms together, give them to the court clerk, who will either put your papers before a judge or tell you when to return for a hearing in front of the judge. Be sure to make multiple copies of your paperwork so that you have a copy on you at all times; you can hand these to law enforcement if need be. Also give a copy to your workplace, school, or where you are staying and to people who are also covered under the restraining order, if your stalker has threatened family members or coworkers. If you have a hearing, know that the judge likely believes you and wants to help you avoid further suffering, but they want to be fair to the abuser too.

Once your restraining order is issued, it is up to you to find someone to deliver the papers to your abuser. You can use a process server (this may cost you money), if one is available in your jurisdiction, or have someone you know over the age of eighteen serve the papers on your abuser. These papers must be served in person; that means you cannot mail or email them to your abuser. Then there is a form the server must file that indicates that they did serve the abuser with the proper paperwork. You will likely see your abuser in court, but law enforcement officials will be there to ensure your safety as well as that of everyone else in the courtroom. If you disagree with a judge's decision, you can always file an appeal to get your restraining order. While this is how the process works in California, most other states follow a similar process. Check the resources section at the end of this text for guidance on getting a restraining order.

Rape, Dating Violence, and Culture

39. How does the media impact our perceptions of rape and dating violence?

The media plays a role in creating what is known as rape culture by an excessive focus on women's and men's bodies, the sexualization of ever-younger females, and by insisting that all men only want one thing from women—sexual activity without commitment. This is problematic on many levels, including the minimization of women's participation in other activities unrelated to their appearance, including sports, academics, and politics; the fetishization of young people's bodies; and the heterosexist normativity that accompanies the idea that all men only want one thing from women. In addition, when the local press or other media expresses greater sympathy for people accused of rape, there appears to be a significant increase in reported rape in that same area afterward. That is not to say that the media coverage causes rape, but it does demonstrate that rape is seen ambiguously at best and condoned or accepted at worst. Research has found that fewer than 5% of news articles use language that reflects rape culture, but when it does, there seems to be less law enforcement investigation of rape charges and less frequent prosecutions. Language that reflects rape culture includes terms such as "nonconsensual sex" or phrases such as "sex with someone who was inebriated." This means that rape culture in the media, in this case local newspapers and news outlets, has real, tangible effects on people in the community.

In addition, movies, video games, music, music videos, and advertisements that perpetuate gender stereotypes of men as dominant and in complete control of their emotions and women as passive, emotional, and meek lead to unconscious acceptance of these outdated and tired norms. Men are seen as aggressive and violent, especially when it comes to sexual activity, while women are portrayed as sexual objects to be won or lost rather than as people with their own complicated relationships with their desires. These tropes also suggest that men lack the emotional capability to nurture others, while it is assumed that every woman comes pre-equipped with the ability to nurture others, especially children, regardless of the reality of their individual capabilities. The truth of the matter is that some men are better nurturers, and some women are much better at working professional jobs or having a lucrative career.

Another way that the media contributes to rape culture is through pornography, or porn. Since porn has become more common in our culture, particularly via the Internet, the norms of porn have also seeped into our culture. While not all porn is violent, there appears to be a tendency toward greater violence, sadism, and rape, sometimes by many men at the same time. The most violent of these pornographic videos are known as "gonzo," and they include elements of sadomasochism. In addition, some things that are common now were uncommon when porn was less widely available, including tattoos, body piercings, and female genital waxing. While these trends are themselves not problematic, many women might be surprised to learn that their tattoo, body piercing, or waxing had its origins in pornography. In addition, continued genital waxing leaves women, visually at least, with bodies that are much more reflective of a prepubescent female rather than an adult female with her own desires and motives for sexual activity. There is also some evidence that continued waxing can lead to permanent hair loss, which may be desirable for some women but might not be for others.

The problem is that this onslaught of sexualized violence is pervasive. Everyone is affected by it to some degree or another if they consume media at all. It is as if media, instead of being a pastime, has become more a part of our everyday lives, and since rape culture is such a big part of what media has to offer, its norms are more and more a part of our lives too. This can also be seen on many college campuses, where fraternities and sororities in particular play a role in objectifying other students, and acting aggressively toward women or using sexualized tropes as part of hazing rituals are ways these students compete with one another. Acting in groups, these students sometimes lose sight of their own personal morality and find themselves part of something that they would not normally be part of. This is particularly the case when alcohol is involved. In addition, as part of hazing, pledges are often asked to do odd sexual activities that are usually designed to humiliate them or their sexual partners. There is some evidence to suggest that men in fraternities are three times more likely to rape than their nonfraternity male peers. Additionally, federal investigators have found some colleges have mishandled cases of rape allegations. If you are in college and in a fraternity or sorority, it would be a good idea to maintain skepticism about activities that seek to humiliate someone or someone's sexual partner.

Additionally, social media platforms provide easy access to rapists and enable them to slut-shame their victims. Along with local newspaper reports that minimize the rape, social media can create a churn of activity, including bullying the victim into silence about the attack that leads to them moving away, dropping out of college, or something much more drastic and lethal. Rape jokes are prevalent in some chat forums, as are celebrations of male aggression and demeaning of sexual partners or victims. While not explicitly condoned, sexualized violence is part of the norm on the Internet, through the media, and as part of our cultural consciousness.

40. What is rape culture?

Rape culture consists of a prevalent attitude that rape is part of life. Rape culture often blames victims for what they wore, what they drank, or who they were with and at what time; suggests that the victim consented; questions their credibility; and demonstrates empathy for the rapist. In addition, rape culture frequently suggests that the victim and rapist had a previous sexual relationship, even though previous sexual activity does not mean every encounter after that was consensual. Other signs of rape culture include questioning the victim's clothing or behavior, including drinking or using illegal drugs. Rape culture includes ideas such as the virgin-whore dyad, as if any woman who has never had sex is morally pure while women who have had sex are sullied or damaged goods. This can be seen in some religious purity circles, where a person who has had sex is compared to a piece of used chewing gum, implying that sexual activity makes one less desirable to the faithful followers of that religion or that the person who has had sex is literally thrown away once they have been used. Rape culture also includes the idea that if a partner has had sex with someone in the past, that makes them less likely to be believed if they are raped later.

Prosecutors likely have a tendency to believe in these and other rape myths, leading to fewer prosecutions than would otherwise happen. In addition, since most prosecutors are elected officials rather than appointed, they seek to protect their conviction rate, and knowing that rapes are infrequently successfully prosecuted means that they are unlikely to prosecute most cases of rape, allowing rapists to plead guilty to lesser charges. Rape culture legitimizes rape and suggests certain standards for rape victims, all while questioning their story and assuming that their claims of rape are likely untrue.

Rape culture includes other less obvious elements, such as rape jokes; acceptance of sexual harassment, including catcalling; a perception that false rape claims are greater than they actually are; teaching women to avoid being raped instead of teaching men to not rape people; and not teaching men to affirm consent throughout a sexual encounter. Rape culture also suggests that men who are raped are weak or less masculine than their peers, and it pressures men to "score," as if sexual activity with a person makes them better while the same act serves to denigrate their sexual partner. Rape culture also suggests that women are submissive and passive during sexual encounters and paradoxically encourages women to not act as if they are hesitant to have sex or as if they are frigid. Rape culture also encourages discussion of women's appearances, as if that is the most important aspect of a woman's life. Slut-shaming is another aspect of rape culture, as is the so-called walk of shame—the walk back to one's own dorm room or home after a night of drinking and sexual activity.

Gender norms contribute to rape culture too. People who fall outside of gender norms are typically shamed, while people who rape are excused, frequently with a boys-will-be-boys attitude toward sexualized violence. In fact, people who are part of the LGBTQIA+ community are at an increased risk of sexual violence when compared to their straight peers, with transgender people being at the highest risk, as more than 66% of transgender people experience sexual violence. In addition, trans people face dating or domestic violence at increased rates as they come out as transgender. Similarly, trans youth face a higher than normal risk of sexual assault during their time in the K–12 educational system, both from other students and from staff at their schools.

Unfortunately, most pornography participates in rape culture as well. Many pornographic products feature rape as a pretense for sexual activity and frequently portray the victim as changing their mind during their attack. With pornography so readily available via the Internet, most people literally have pornography available at their fingertips, informing them about sexual activity and consent. In addition, there is little pornography available that features sexual activity that is consensual and does not include some element of violence or aggression, either verbal or physical. In fact, consuming pornography typically leads to a person having particular expectations regarding sexual activity, and there is some evidence that people who consume pornography are found to be dating or domestically violent with their partner at higher than usual rates. This does not mean that every porn consumer will necessarily become violent domestically or while dating or that they will commit sexual assault or rape. If you and your partner enjoy porn together and have found healthy ways to incorporate that into your lives, great. Otherwise, this might be taken as a warning that future harmful acts may occur.

41. What is victim blaming?

While victim blaming is common to dating and domestic violence and sexual assault and rape cases, it is not common in other sorts of criminal activity. The idea of blaming a victim of burglary for what they were wearing, drinking, or eating makes clear how ridiculous this behavior is, as none of us would consider blaming someone for their home or car being robbed. In cases of dating or domestic violence and sexual assault and rape cases, victim blaming questions what a victim was eating, drinking, doing, saying, and wearing or where the victim was located at the time of their victimization. Pretty much any sort of choice the victim made on the day they were attacked is called into question as well as their historical relationship with their attacker. At the same time, victim blaming allows the attacker to escape judgment, as if the victim's choices naturally led to the attack rather than the attacker deciding to attack someone. The purpose of victim blaming appears to be a shift in judgment so that the victim becomes, in essence, an attacker rather than the other way around. This also helps create empathy for the attacker and doubt about the victim's claims of being attacked.

Victim blaming leads to lower rates of reported rapes, sexual assaults, and dating and domestic violence, as victims know implicitly or explicitly that their victimization will call nearly all of their choices into question. In addition, victim blaming also means that other people feel a false sense of security, as if their choices mean that they will not be victimized—as if that could ever be guaranteed. Victim blaming can lead to a sort of checklist mentality: did I lock the door, did I notify friends where I am going, or other sorts of efforts to protect oneself. In addition, the media presentation and sensationalization of rape myths lead to a sense in some communities that perpetrators should be treated more leniently or absolved completely of their crimes, especially if they are athletes, as if the victim sent out signals that they wanted to be attacked. While this is a ridiculous practice that defies logic, it does the work of rape culture in ensuring that victims maintain their silence after they have been attacked.

Victim blaming is more than just what happens when a victim comes forward with their story of being assaulted in local media reports. Social media plays a role too. When victims tell their stories, all too often, people on social media begin bullying the victim, blaming them for the attack and questioning their morals, motivations, and life choices. In addition, social media helps rumors of sexual promiscuity spread more quickly, leading to assumptions of promiscuity rather than rape or that this is another instance of what is known as postcoital regret. In addition, jokes that reinforce the belief that victims ask to be attacked lead to lower rates of reporting dating and domestic violence, sexual assault, and rape. But it does not have to be this way.

Research shows that a victim believing or educational model of digital activism can reverse much of the stigma associated with being a victim of dating or domestic violence, sexual assault, or rape. Activism around slut-shaming, as that is what social media shaming of victims is termed, via so-called SlutWalks appears to reduce the stigma of reporting sexual assaults or rapes in communities that have this sort of activity. At times, it seems that newspapers' reporting of sexual assault and rape tends to perpetuate a victim-blaming culture, while social media accounts may tend to focus on the victim's rights in the right atmosphere and social media's role in bringing about justice—all elements that are frequently left out of the local television and newspaper reports.

In addition, there is a mindset called the just-world theory that posits that bad things happen to bad people; this means that most people who think of themselves as good people can rest assured that their choices will not lead to their being victimized by other people. This sort of mindset is a form of victim blaming and works to shift the focus to what the victim did to cause the assault. This mindset also reinforces ideas of stranger danger, or the notion that the only way a so-called good person would be assaulted would be to be in a dark alley by oneself and being attacked by a complete stranger. The data proves that the danger is all too close to home, as most people who are survivors of dating or domestic violence, sexual assault, or rape are attacked by people they know and typically by someone they know well. This mindset also hypothesizes that victims fall into two categories: virgins and whores. Virgins are seen as people who would never be raped, as if they could not be, while whores are seen as people who want it; they are promiscuous and only lie about it when they claim they were victims of dating or domestic violence, sexual assault, or rape. Either way, victims of dating and domestic violence, sexual assault, and rape are the big losers in rape culture.

42. What is the #MeToo movement about?

Tarana Burke coined the phrase "Me Too" in 2006 as an attempt to help girls and women who were survivors of sexual assault. The idea behind the phrase is empowerment through empathy and community; that is, if a person talks about their sexual assault or rape, it may help others speak about their own victimization. The term was infrequently used until 2017, when actress Ashley Judd accused Harvey Weinstein of sexually assaulting her. Later that year, Alyssa Milano tweeted, "If you've been sexually harassed or assaulted write '#me too' as a reply to this tweet."

As a result, later that year, gymnast McKayla Maroney accused Dr. Larry Nassar, then the U.S. Olympic gymnastics team doctor, of sexually assaulting her. Even more survivors came forward, accusing people such as actor Kevin Spacey, Republican Senate candidate Roy Moore, comedian Louis C. K., NBC *Today* show host Matt Lauer, NPR's *Prairie Home Companion* host Garrison Keillor, Def Jam cofounder Russell Simmons, U.S. senator Al Franken, director Woody Allen, television chef Mario Batali, and theater prodigy Gary Goddard. On January 1, 2018, over 300 women of Hollywood formed the coalition against harassment called Time's Up. At the 75th Golden Globes that year, many celebrities wore black in support of the Time's Up movement or Time's Up pins on their clothing. At that Golden Globes event, Oprah Winfrey's acceptance speech for the Cecil B. DeMille award included a statement about the power of women standing up against sexual harassment and rape, and she noted that it is a problem that is nationwide rather than one confined to the entertainment industry. A few days later, in a *Los Angeles Times* interview, five women accused actor James Franco of inappropriate or exploitive behavior when he was their teacher or mentor. On January 20 of that year, millions marched in the second Women's March, protesting Donald Trump's inauguration and the history of sexual assault and rape claims against him and encouraging others to register to vote.

Actor Jeremy Piven was accused of sexual assault by three women initially and then another three women came forward with their own separate claims against him. In a *New York Times* interview, actress Uma Thurman alleges that Harvey Weinstein forced her to have sex with him in London, and she accused Quentin Tarantino of forcing her to drive a car she believed was faulty and of spitting and choking her during the filming of *Kill Bill*. Country star Vince Gill showcased a song about sexual assault and survival at Nashville's Country Radio Showcase, noting that people now have the courage to talk about their assault, and he shared his own experience of being sexually assaulted as a youth. Monica Lewinsky shared that while she had viewed her relationship with then President Bill Clinton as a consensual one, her understanding of the relationship had changed as a result of the #MeToo movement, which also focuses on the power differential between the aggressor and survivor.

In March 2018, at the Academy Awards, host Jimmy Kimmel made fun of Harvey Weinstein as a sexual predator, and Ashley Judd, Annabella Sciorra, and Salma Hayek spoke about the changes being wrought as a result of the accusations against Harvey Weinstein, saying that "new voices, different voices . . . joining in a mighty chorus that is finally saying 'time's up.'" That same month saw the firing of Metropolitan Opera conductor James Levin after several men alleged that he had sexually abused and harassed them. Later that March, the investigation into U.S. Olympic gymnastics team doctor Larry Nassar found that a dean at Michigan State University, where Nassar worked as a professor in the College of Human Medicine, protected Nassar rather than following up with the gymnasts and their complaints of sexual assault during routine physical examinations. *The New York Times* and *The New Yorker* both received Pulitzer prizes for their investigative journalism surrounding the Harvey Weinstein case.

A massage therapist accused Stan Lee of fondling himself and inappropriately grabbing her during a massage at a Chicago hotel in 2017. On April 26, 2018, Bill Cosby was found guilty of drugging and molesting a Toronto woman in one of the first cases to come to trial during the era of the #MeToo movement; since that time, Cosby's conviction has been overturned. A war correspondent for NBC News alleged that Tom Brokaw made inappropriate sexual advances to her in an attempt to have an affair. Spotify announced in May 2018 that it would no longer include R & B artist R. Kelly's songs on their playlists; his music would be available but not promoted on the site as a result of allegations that he has a long history of abusing women, in particular women under the age of eighteen, starting with his marriage in 1994 to singer Aaliyah, who was then fifteen years old and lied about her age on the couple's marriage license.

In September 2018, Christine Blasey Ford accused U.S. Supreme Court nominee Brett Kavanaugh of sexual assault when they were both high schoolers in Bethesda, Maryland. Initially, Blasey Ford sent a letter with her concerns to Democratic senator Dianne Feinstein and asked for anonymity, but she later outed herself in a *Washington Post* article; the letter was later released by Senator Chuck Grassley, a Republican lawmaker from Iowa, who was given the letter by Feinstein. Despite Blasey Ford moving testimony before the judiciary committee, Kavanaugh was approved as a candidate and later inaugurated as a Supreme Court justice. Later that year, the House Ethics Committee urged a change in how sexual harassment and other abusive behaviors are treated on Capitol Hill, with legislators no longer allowed to use their congressional budgets for official business to pay off sexual harassment accusers.

In December 2018, several women accused Neil deGrasse Tyson of sexual assault and harassment. In January 2019, the Lifetime network aired the miniseries *Surviving R. Kelly*, a documentary outlining the scope of the allegations against the R & B superstar. Several men accused *X-Men* director Bryan Singer of having sex with them when they were young men. Seven women accused singer-songwriter Ryan Adams of offering to help them with their careers but turning things sexual when they were alone, often becoming verbally and emotionally abusive. In addition, Ellen DeGeneres appeared on an episode of Netflix's *My Next Guest Needs No Introduction with David Letterman* series and described her abuse at the hands of her stepfather in hopes of encouraging young people to come forward with their own stories of being abused or assaulted.

In July 2018, hedge fund manager Jeffrey Epstein faced accusations of abusing over a dozen girls aged fourteen years old and up. Epstein was accused of offering money for massages and then molesting the girls at his homes in Florida and New York. Numerous other celebrities were implicated in the abuse of young women because of their association with Epstein, notably including Microsoft founder Bill Gates. Several women accused Placido Domingo, the famed opera singer, of offering to help them with their careers and then pressuring them into sexual relationships and retaliating against them when his advances were spurned.

Overall, the goal of the #MeToo movement was to provide support for victims of sexual assault and rape and in particular to call out unwanted sexual advances by people in power, especially when their victims were women of color or underage.

43. What is a SlutWalk? How do I start one?

A SlutWalk is typically a campus-based activity that seeks to expose the double standard when it comes to female sexuality. Instead of participating in the frequent slut-shaming that our rape culture typically does after accusations of sexual assault or rape, a SlutWalk is activism to increase awareness about the real causes of sexual assault and rape—people who do not respect other people's boundaries. The protest movement began in 2011 after a Toronto police officer said that women who do not want to be raped should "avoid dressing like sluts." In addition, by their very public nature, SlutWalks work to reclaim spaces that objectify everyone—as objects for desire, derision, or worse.

SlutWalks are intersectional, meaning that they support people from the LGBTQIA+ community, people of all races, people in the disabled community, sex workers, and others who do not fit neatly into societal labels. SlutWalks ask participants to imagine a world where all bodies are respected and all sex is consensual. Part of the work of a SlutWalk is reclaiming the word *slut*, turning it from a term intended to shame the person it is used against into a moment of solidarity across differences. In this way, the SlutWalk does similar work to what the gay rights movement did by taking what had been a slur and turning it into public and political action that defuses the slur, making it commonplace rather than incendiary. In addition, SlutWalks also welcome people whose work is considered sex work, such as prostitutes, strippers, and other sex workers, as they are often victims of slut-shaming behaviors, especially when they come forward with claims of rape or sexual assault. It should be noted that not everyone is on board with reclaiming the term *slut*; in fact, a group of Black female academics, activists, and writers has argued that embracing the term reinforces many of the tropes about Black women and their sexuality, and as Black women, they do not have the privilege of embracing the term. However, SlutWalks have been touted as the most successful feminist movement activity of the last twenty years.

To begin your own campus or community SlutWalk, you will need to organize with your student government, faculty, and on-campus events coordinators. Reaching out to your on-campus Title IX office would also be a good place to begin organizing a SlutWalk, as they have a plethora of resources and suggestions for making the event successful. While SlutWalks around the world have focused on different issues, the theme remains the same: rape is caused by rapists rather than anything that their victims do or do not do. SlutWalks emphasize education of cisgender heterosexual males that cisgender females' and everyone else's bodies are not there for their pleasure and that their opinion about anyone else's body is intrusive and unwelcome.

If you are putting together a community-based SlutWalk, consider reaching out to people at the local college or university or reach out to leaders within your community. This can include police, clergy, and teachers at your own school but also local media people, who can help get the word out about your event. Many communities have a community calendar; consider putting your activity there along with posting flyers announcing the day and time of the event. In addition, utilize social media that people older than you might use, including Facebook. Lots of folks over the age of thirty do not check their Instagram, WhatsApp, or Snapchat accounts frequently enough for a post there to be as effective as it could be. Be sure to secure approval through your local city or county government if the SlutWalk is moving through any public spaces, such as downtown streets or toward a public park, so that you can ensure a safe event for all participants.

Case Studies

1. JENNA HAS AN ABUSIVE BOYFRIEND

Jenna's relationship with her boyfriend, Mike, started innocently enough. They met at school, and she thought he was really cute, funny, and charming. They began spending more and more time together after school, initially as study buddies, either at her house or his. As they became closer to one another, they changed their study dates to whoever's house had no one at home after school. Eventually, he asked her out, and she eagerly said yes. He was an attentive boyfriend and seemed to know what she wanted before she did.

Initially, Mike was respectful of Jenna's boundaries in terms of physical contact but was always pushing her limits. A goodnight kiss eventually turned into an expectation of extended kissing and touching each other intimately. Eventually, she gave in to his pressure and consented to sexual activity, even though it was her first time. After that first sexual encounter, Mike assumed that they would have sex every time they went out together, and at first Jenna believed that this was now part of the deal too. She figured that since he had dated other people in the past, he knew what a dating relationship should be like and that he was treating her the same way he would any girlfriend. She liked having sex with him but sometimes just wanted things to go back to the way they were before they had sex so that they could go out and do other things without necessarily having sex. What happened instead was that the only time Mike did not expect to have sex with Jenna was when she was having her period.

Instead of basing their relationship on study sessions, Mike began demeaning Jenna, acting as if she was unintelligent, and he called her stupid in front of his friends. As their relationship progressed past the three-month mark, he became more and more demanding, wanting to know where she was when he was not around, who she was hanging out with, and whether she was texting or talking to other people. He became increasingly jealous and controlling and wanted to keep tabs on her whenever they were apart. He demanded to see her cell phone for text messages with other people.

Recently, Jenna refused to tell him where she had been, and he threatened to punch her if she did not. She relented and told him she had been at a girlfriend's house. He apologized to her and said that he would never hurt her and that he loved her too much to do that. Jenna loved the closeness she felt after he apologized, and he gave her a long hug without demanding sexual activity.

When Jenna described this event to her closest friend, Adam, he was horrified that Jenna was being manipulated into sexual activity and controlled, especially now that there were threats of physical violence. Adam suggested that they go to the school counselor together. Jenna refused Adam's offer at first, worried about what Mike would think if he found out. After another blowup when Mike threatened to push her out of his moving car, Jenna promised Mike that she would tell him where she was at all times, and Mike joked that he would never push her out of the car and that he loved her too much to do that. Jenna was embarrassed and ashamed, but she told Adam what had happened and agreed to go with him to talk to the counselor. Once they were in the counselor's office, the counselor closed the door and asked Jenna if she wanted Adam to stay, and she said yes.

The counselor first asked Jenna whether she felt safe talking to him, and Jenna hesitatingly agreed that she did. The counselor asked Jenna to talk about her relationship with Mike, how they met, and how they began dating. Jenna told the counselor that Mike was warm, friendly, and funny when they first met. Jenna related that their relationship soon became about sexual activity, that Mike came to expect that they would have sex every time they went out together, and that she was not always interested in having sex but did enjoy the cuddling afterward. Then Jenna described her experience with Mike's threatening behavior and how that had her pretty scared.

At that point, the counselor pulled out a graphic depiction of what is known as the cycle of abuse, or the power and control wheel. The counselor went over what the cycle is, how it operates—with tension building after a period of happiness for the couple, then an outburst, and then contrition or saying sorry for the harm a person may have done, and then a period of happiness again; so much of what he said resonated with Jenna. The cycle of abuse seemed to match pretty closely with Jenna's experiences with Mike. Jenna saw that Mike's jokes about her intellect were part of the cycle of abuse, as he sought to reduce her self-esteem. She also noted that his demanding to know her whereabouts was part of the cycle too, as he tried to isolate her from her other friends.

The counselor suggested that Jenna see a psychologist to follow up with her and help her as she transitioned out of the relationship with Mike. Jenna hesitatingly agreed to see a psychologist, and her counselor arranged an appointment for her with a local psychologist.

While Jenna was troubled by what she learned, she continued going out with her boyfriend while she waited for her first appointment with the psychologist. He was her first boyfriend, and she thought they would always be together—that is what they promised one another the first time they had sex, after all. She had already envisioned how life with him would be as adults living together, but she slowly began to realize that she had built that make-believe life based only on the times when he was good to her.

When it was time for her session with the psychologist, she asked Jenna to outline her experiences with Mike and what had brought her to the counselor's office in the first place. Jenna described her relationship with Mike, his escalating demands, and going to the school counselor, who went over the cycle of abuse with her and suggested that she meet with a psychologist. Jenna was nervous and appeared ready to back out of counseling with the psychologist, as Mike had once more said that he respected her and her choices. The psychologist asked whether there was any drug or alcohol use by either Mike or Jenna; although they were both under the legal age for any of those substances, Jenna admitted that they had both used alcohol in the past.

After several more conversations with the psychologist in which she talked about her experiences dating Mike, Jenna decided that it was best if she and her boyfriend stopped seeing one another. Mike took the news really hard; he had thought they were working on their relationship and felt betrayed that Jenna never told him that she was talking to a psychologist about their relationship. He even threatened to commit suicide if Jenna broke up with him, but Jenna was prepared for this; her psychologist had told her that emotional blackmail is a common tactic when an abuser sees his victim leaving.

Jenna's background, coming from a conservative family that urged children to remain so-called pure until marriage, meant that Jenna felt uncomfortable talking about her experiences with her parents, who were otherwise typically supportive. Because she and Mike had engaged in sexual activity, Jenna worried that her parents would think of her as damaged or less valuable than she otherwise might have been. In fact, at a youth group meeting some time ago, a youth minister had compared people who have had sex prior to marriage as being similar to used chewing gum— something no one would want.

Analysis

Jenna's relationship problem with Mike is all too common. Many young adults find themselves in dating relationships that start out fine but turn out disastrously wrong. With most young adult dating relationships, there are several red flags prior to the threats of violence: demanding to know a partner's whereabouts is a sign of feeling insecure about the relationship and demonstrates a desire to control the partner. In addition, belittling a partner in front of friends can frequently be an attempt to make that person feel like a big shot and is intended to make the victim feel bad about themselves and to identify more closely with the abuser.

Instead, young couples would do well to brainstorm together their guidelines for a dating relationship and to talk about what to do if one of them crossed a line. Young adults who find themselves in a dating relationship that has become violent or where there have been threats of violence also need to learn to stand up for themselves and to talk to school counselors, parents, and friends about their experiences, trusting that these people have their best interests in mind. Without Adam's help, Jenna likely would not have gone to the school counselor in the first place and definitely would not have called what was happening between her and her boyfriend violence. Jenna learned some valuable lessons, but her heart still ached for the boyfriend she once felt so close to.

Having a family history of conservative values, and particularly the culture of purity in regard to sexual activity, makes people more prone to hiding sexual activity from parents and many of the other supportive people in their lives. Frequently, young people feel as though they cannot trust most of the adults in their lives, especially if the issue involves their sexuality, and instead confide in a close friend. Many victims of dating violence never tell anyone else about what is going on in their relationships. Some 40% of girls surveyed, ages fourteen to seventeen years old, responded that they knew of someone who had been hit or beaten by a partner.

A high school counselor may provide young adults with some tools to think about in regard to their relationships, but more importantly, a good high school counselor will also suggest that they talk to a psychologist. Speaking with a psychologist can help a young adult see more clearly that their experience is abusive and can help prepare them for potential reactions when the relationship ends.

While many of these abusive relationships end with both members of the couple doing relatively well, the impact of an early abusive relationship can resonate throughout their lives if they fail to remember the red flags of abuse. Teen dating violence has an impact on a young person's ability to succeed in high school, can increase dissatisfaction with their bodies, can increase risks of suicidal thinking and behavior, and lead to substance abuse, including binge drinking and drug use. Other potential negative impacts of an abusive dating relationship include poor performance or dropping out of high school, skipping classes, increased feelings of worthlessness, increased sensitivity to friendly touch, drug abuse, self-mutilation or destructive behavior, and STDs. In fact, early abusive intimate relationships leave victims twice as likely to have abusive relationships with others later in life.

While some adults might minimize early dating relationships, in some ways, they lay the foundation for what a person seeks in a partner and can influence a person's choices over their lifetime, especially if there is not also a period of deep reflection of what they want and need out of a relationship along with a realization that they deserve to be happy.

2. NORA WAS RAPED BY HER BOYFRIEND

Nora is a trans high school student. Nora's relationship with her boyfriend began normally enough: they met through a couple of their friends when everyone was hanging out at another friend's house. David asked for her number and texted her the next day, asking her out for coffee. From there, they began seeing more and more of one another, and they seemed to get along really well. David took their relationship seriously from the beginning and always treated Nora like a lady. He opened doors for her, told her how lucky he was, and took her to meet his parents. She had worried as she began transitioning that she might never find someone who loves her as she is rather than expecting her to be something she is not. But with David, all those worries seemed to evaporate. Sometimes it felt as if she were living through a romantic movie, one where the couple falls in love and stays together for the rest of their lives. She felt she was the luckiest girl in the world to have such a wonderful boyfriend and imagined that if things went well, they might build a life with one another, just like in those movies she had seen. They seemed to have the same interests in movies, books, and video games, and being together felt natural and easy.

All of that changed last night, and now Nora is questioning everything about their relationship. Their date began normally enough. They ordered takeout for delivery and watched their favorite series together—the one they had been looking forward to all week. After the meal, they cleaned up the kitchen as they usually did. Nora washed the few dishes they had dirtied, and David dried and took out the trash. There did not seem to be any tension or expectation of intimacy; David was just as he usually was—affable, friendly, and caring. That all changed pretty quickly after they played their video game and Nora beat David pretty soundly. David appeared to be taking the loss a little bit more seriously than usual, and Nora joked that he did not like being beaten by a girl. He sulked for a while but eventually appeared to get over the loss. When he began kissing Nora, she did not think anything of it, as they did that all the time after they had played video games or hung out together.

Nora did not feel like having sex last night, and she told David that, adding that it had been a long day and she was too tired to have sex. David kept on kissing her and touching her, and she repeatedly said that she did not want to have sex. David was undeterred and kept touching and kissing Nora until they eventually had sex anyway.

Although Nora did not physically fight back against her boyfriend's intimacy, she did protest that she did not want to have sex. Since he continued with sexual activity and ignored her protests, what happened to Nora was certainly rape, even though they had previously had sex. If she did not consent, regardless of whether they had been intimate with one another previously, and regardless of Nora's being transgender, then what happened between them was rape.

Nora had some decisions to make about her rape. First, should she tell her boyfriend, David, that he had raped her? Nora imagined that would not go over too well and felt certain he would claim that she wanted it. Should she tell anyone else about her rape? The thought of involving medical professionals in her situation made her uncomfortable, as she had encountered medical professionals who do not understand how to treat transgender people in the past, and that was just for routine medical care. How much worse would she be treated if she went in and said she had been raped? Does she file rape charges against him? How would that go? Nora has a hard time imagining that law enforcement officers would treat her with the respect, empathy, and kindness she deserved, much less speak to David and attempt to hold him accountable. Should she tell the friends they have in common? If she did that, she would risk losing the best group of friends she had had since she began transitioning.

Ultimately, Nora decided to tell her best friend, Angela, what happened. Angela listened to Nora's story carefully, told Nora that what she had experienced was rape, and suggested that she call the transgender abuse hotline (see the resources section for trans folks). Nora felt better after talking to the advocates at the hotline, who understood what had happened to her and treated her with respect and empathy. Nora decided afterward to break up with her boyfriend.

Analysis

Unfortunately, Nora's problems with her boyfriend are all too common for transgender people. In fact, more than half of transgender people report activity that can be considered dating violence. Many male-to-female trans folks find themselves in situations with heterosexual partners who either have or develop homophobia and strike out at their partners in an attempt to demonstrate to themselves, if no one else, that they are still manly. It is likely that Nora's boyfriend was feeling less masculine than his peers, and he raped Nora as a way of demonstrating that he is aggressively heterosexual.

Unfortunately, trans people's skepticism about going for medical care after an assault is well founded. Nearly half of trans folks face discrimination when they attempted to get health care, and that number increases to nearly 80% for trans people of color. A quarter of trans people report that they delay health care because of the discrimination and disrespect they have experienced in the past. Similarly, police officers are also ill equipped to work with trans people. Half of transgender people report being hesitant to contact law enforcement, and a quarter of transgender people report experiencing harassment; these numbers are higher for transgender people of color.

Patriarchal cultural norms suggested that men were dominant and women were dominated. Violence against women, whether transgender or cisgender, was seen as less of a problem than violence of men against other men. As a root cause, patriarchal culture, including the movies, shows, books, and other media we all consume, taught young men and women that violence against women was routine, somewhat to be expected, and that it should not be a big problem. While some women have perpetrated intimate partner violence, the consequences for women who are victims of intimate partner violence experience greater trauma, physically, mentally, and socially. There is also some evidence to suggest that intimate partner violence is also more common among impoverished people and people of color, especially in places where inequality has been unacknowledged.

Part of the problem that transgender people have faced include deadnaming, or using the person's previous misgendered name, whether at school or on public documents. In addition, trans people also frequently experienced violence at the hands of medical professionals, including unwanted psychiatric examinations, unwanted surgeries, and forced sterilization. The justification for these horrific behaviors has been the fact that until recently, trans people were thought to have a mental illness; in fact, the fifth edition of the *Diagnostic and Statistical Manual of Mental Disorders* (DSMV-5) was the first to categorize trans people as having body dysphoria or distress that their gender does not match what society considered appropriate. Prior to that, being transsexual was seen as a mental illness. The problem of deadnaming is related to the medical violence trans people experience: deadnaming implies that the trans person is wrong about their gender identity and that the state has always known better what their gender has been.

In addition to problems of intimate partner violence, trans folks have faced an increased risk of street harassment and sexual assault, and those numbers are higher for trans folks of color. In addition to intimate partner violence, street harassment, and sexual assault, trans folks are also at increased risks for homelessness, with over half of respondents to one survey reporting homelessness.

3. DANIEL DOESN'T LIKE BEING PUNCHED BY HIS GIRLFRIEND

Daniel and his girlfriend, Alisha, had been going together pretty steadily for a while and spent most of their free time together during school lunch breaks and sometimes at each other's houses after school. They had met in sixth grade and began seeing one another outside of school at the end of last year. Since they began going to a new middle school in the fall, they have been spending more time together—both in school and otherwise. Last year, Daniel walked behind Alisha as they walked home, but that changed after winter break, when they began walking home next to one another. Eventually, they started holding hands on their walk home from school as they talked about their day at school, the latest about the mean girl in gym class, and the goofy kids in band class. She was the first girlfriend Daniel had ever had, and he really liked her. They have similar interests in band and video games, and he felt as if he could talk to her about anything and she would not judge him or think he was weird. As they talked and joked around, Alisha sometimes punched him on his bicep when he said something she found hilarious. He liked that she found him funny, but he did not like being hit. He liked her a lot but was not comfortable telling her to stop punching him, as he was afraid she would think less of him or that he was too weak and break up with him.

Daniel struggled to find someone he could talk to and eventually confided in his older brother, Jeremy. Jeremy is only three years older than Daniel, and Daniel had always looked to him for guidance or when he had an issue and did not want to talk to his parents first. Jeremy told him that he was in a similar situation when he was Daniel's age and that these sorts of behaviors are pretty common when people are first learning how to be with someone they like. Jeremy congratulated Daniel on having a girlfriend and asked about how their relationship began. Daniel outlined their walks home, how he followed Alisha the first half of last school year, that they began walking together after winter break, and that they had begun holding hands just this fall at about the same time that they began spending a lot more time together. Daniel also told Jeremy about how much he liked Alisha and that he does not want her to break up with him.

Jeremy told Daniel that a lot more people are having similar experiences than Daniel thinks and that nearly a third of all people who are in dating relationships experience dating violence. Jeremy suggested that Daniel do three things: first, tell his girlfriend to stop hitting him or he will have to break up with her; second, tell his parents about what has been going on; and third, speak with the school counselor about it so that he can find resources to help him work on developing healthy intimate relationships rather than abusive ones.

In addition, Jeremy and Daniel come from a domestically violent home, and Jeremy is Daniel's primary caregiver after school. Jeremy also has his own girlfriend, and they spend a fair amount of time in his room with the door closed when they are at Jeremy's house. Jeremy and Daniel's parents fight one another physically, but they have not hit their children. There have been times when their mother has called the police to intervene and other times when their father has called them. Neither one of their parents has ever chosen to press charges, and so the police reports went nowhere. Coming from a domestically violent home puts both of the boys at an increased risk of violent intimate relationships, with their being either the victim or the aggressor. While both of them are typically pretty good kids, they spend a significant part of the day without adult supervision.

The next afternoon, Daniel told Alisha how much he liked her and that he hoped they would continue as boyfriend and girlfriend, but he would appreciate it if she stopped hitting him when she thinks he has said something funny. Alisha listened to Daniel carefully and apologized for hitting him, saying that she had seen other girls doing that to their boyfriends and did not realize that it was inappropriate. She promised to work on not hitting him anymore, and they continued to see one another. Daniel waited to tell his parents, as he felt that the timing was not quite right; after all, they did not even know he had a girlfriend. Instead, he went to the school counselor for advice and told him about his experiences.

Analysis

Daniel's problem with his girlfriend is more common than many people might think. Unfortunately, the majority of these young people never confide in anyone about the abuse they have experienced, and there is some evidence to suggest that young men are less likely than their female peers to report dating violence to anyone, likely because of the perception that strong men can take it, even though their bodies hurt just like anyone else's.

In fact, according to the Centers for Disease Control and Prevention (CDC), one in nine female teens and one in thirteen male teens experience some form of dating violence. While some adults might consider thirteen years old to be too young to date, over 70% of young people between the ages of thirteen and fourteen consider themselves part of a dating couple. Violent behavior between dating couples frequently begins between the sixth and twelfth grades and can have impacts on adult intimate relationships if not resolved with the partner or by having a therapist, counselor, or other trusted adult to talk to.

There are four types of dating violence: physical, sexual, psychological, and stalking, either in person or virtually. Some 33% of young adults report being victimized by sexual, verbal, physical, or emotional dating violence. It is important to take these incidents seriously and to treat them as the problems they are, as there are numerous consequences for dating violence and the potential for getting into fights with other people, bringing weapons to school, or considering suicide. There are legal options too, if the abuse is severe enough, although several states do not recognize dating violence as domestic violence, leaving young adults without recourse with a restraining order to keep the abuser away from their victim. Frequently, there can also be a diminution in self-confidence, a fear to express one's feelings, shame and guilt, depression, anxiety, and feelings of isolation or loneliness.

4. BRIANNA ISN'T SURE IF SHE WAS RAPED IN VEGAS

Brianna just turned twenty-one and went with friends to Las Vegas to celebrate. Brianna and her friends had drunk alcohol before, so she had thought she could handle a night of partying in Vegas. They had gone to one another's homes when the parents were out and drank their alcohol; sometimes it seemed as if drinking was the one thing that kept their friend group together. The trip to Vegas was Aimee's idea; Brianna is the youngest person in their friend group, and everyone wanted to show her a good time. Since Aimee came up with the idea months ahead of time, everyone saved money to afford their hotel rooms and to take care of all the other expenses related to the trip.

The group began by pregaming—drinking prior to going out—with tequila. There was a lot of alcohol and rowdiness at the bar they found as everyone celebrated with Brianna. They started out buying pitchers of beer but soon switched to taking shots of tequila. At this point, a group of men at the bar discovered that it was Brianna's birthday celebration and bought the group a round of tequila shots. They ordered the shots from the bartender and brought them on a tray to the group. Sometime later, Brianna was dancing with a cute guy from the group that had bought them shots, and he invited her up to his room. He was a really good dancer, and she felt attracted to him. But she knew that she should be careful around people she does not know well. She remembers walking to the elevator with him but cannot remember anything else, including whether she had sex with him.

One of Brianna's friends, Lauren, suggested that if she thought she was raped that she might want to go to the local emergency room so that medical professionals could use a rape kit to collect potential evidence of her possible assault. Brianna worried about what her other friends and family might think of her when she returned home, but Lauren convinced her to go when she said she would go with her and help her through the process. When Brianna arrived at the hospital, she was surprised at how friendly and empathic the medical professionals were. They asked her a few simple questions, such as her name, age, address, and whether she had any insurance coverage that should be billed. They asked her to sign a Health Insurance Portability and Accountability Act (HIPAA) form, which allowed her to share or keep her information confidential. That made her feel a lot better about having decided to go to the ER; she did not have to worry about family or friends finding out what had happened unless she decided to tell them.

Once Brianna was in the exam room, she was asked to take off all her clothes and was offered a hospital gown to wear during her examination. Lauren stayed with her and held her hand through parts of the examination when Brianna was scared. The medical professional who performed the exam was friendly and asked very few questions. The one Brianna remembered most was the one about whether she thought the man she met was wearing a condom. Because she could not remember, she assumed he had not, and she was offered medication to treat potential sexually transmitted diseases and the so-called morning-after pill, or Plan B (available at most pharmacies without a prescription) to prevent any potential pregnancy from attaching to the inside of her uterus.

Brianna was surprised when she learned that she could not have her clothes back, but she was offered alternate clothing for her ride back to the hotel, where she and her friends would check out and go home. Brianna had a little bit of time to think about whether she should attempt to file charges against the man at the nightclub, but she was not sure that she knew where to find him or knew much about him other than his first name.

Analysis

Brianna and her friends made some mistakes when they went out that night, but that does not mean that Brianna caused what may have happened to her. Unfortunately, this experience is all too common. There are plenty of people out there who appear normal, even nice, who turn out to be the type of people who drug others so that they can have sex with them. Most frequently, these drugs are used along with alcohol, as alcohol makes a person's inhibitions lower all by itself. Most date rape drugs, also known as club drugs because that is where they are most often used, are typically tasteless and colorless, meaning that you cannot detect them if they are put into your drink. The exception is Rohypnol, which also used to be colorless, but since its use as a date rape drug became better known, drug manufacturers have been making it green with a dark blue core. When the drug dissolves, it turns beverages blue, although some generic manufacturers do not necessarily take this extra step to warn potential victims.

When celebrating or partying with friends, it is advisable to adopt a buddy system or a way for friends to ensure that everyone stays safe.

Sometimes that means having a designated driver, while other times it means that everyone comes as a group and leaves as a group. Whichever approach your group takes, special care should be taken with beverages. Watch your friends' beverages when they go to the restroom and ask them to watch yours when it is your turn. Covering your beverage with your hand is an additional way to stay safe, as it is easy enough to drop a substance into a beverage while a person looks elsewhere. It is also a good idea to avoid consuming beverages that you have not witnessed being poured, or that are handed to you by someone other than a bartender or waiter. While it is true that most rapes occur between people who already know one another, it is also true that there are people who prey on people who visit nightclubs, particularly nightclubs frequented by tourists, as they are perceived as less likely to report a sexual assault or rape.

5. JAMES WONDERS ABOUT ROMEO AND JULIET LAWS

James and Janine met because James's friend was dating Janine's older sister, Karolyn. James's friend, Robbie, met Karolyn at his part-time job, where James also works, so it was natural that James and Robbie would pop in after work sometimes to chat with Karolyn. That is where James met Janine. She was as pretty as Karolyn and seemed intelligent but was not stuck up about it. James asked Karolyn about Janine at work the next time they had a shift together and learned that Janine had just turned sixteen a couple of months ago, that she is on the honor roll, and that she is a sophomore in the same high school where James went. Since James is already over the age of eighteen, he worries about putting himself in legal jeopardy by dating a younger person. He also does not want to be thought of as someone who would take advantage of someone younger than him.

James began his search by reading about Romeo and Juliet laws in this book, and then he flipped to the resources section at the end of the book. There he found a resource that looked promising, and he looked up his state's laws on dating underage people, where he discovered that his state's age of consent is sixteen years old. However, he was still worried about being criminally liable if he and Janine began having sex. He also saw that over half of U.S. states have no Romeo and Juliet provision, which would make a statutory rape claim against him a misdemeanor rather than a felony. He asked Robbie what he thought he should do. He really liked Janine and imagined they would be a great couple, but he did not want to put himself in any legal danger. Robbie suggested that they look at sites that talk about building healthy relationships to see whether beginning a relationship with Janine made sense. They learned that there are some warnings for people beginning relationships with someone older or younger, but most of the advice focused on people who are already over the age of eighteen. One thing that did help was a suggestion to build a profile of what a person wants in a relationship.

Generally speaking, most people want more out of an intimate relationship than just sex, so thinking about the fundamental elements a person wants in a relationship makes sense—at any age. It is not nearly enough that a couple shares a preference in music genres, artists, or extracurricular activities. It is also important that people who decide to get together share some common values, such as honesty, hard work, caring for other people, and working toward long-term goals, such as going to college.

Next, James and his friend learned that they should query their potential partners to see whether their fundamental elements line up with their own and what their long-term goals are. Things to consider include, Will either of them go to college? If so, where? Would they try to go to the same school or try to make a long-distance relationship work? After college, what do they want out of life? Do they want to move away from their hometown? Or are they content at home but want a more professional life than their parents had? Would either of them consider having children? How firm are they about that topic? How do they handle money? Is one a spender and the other a saver? What about household chores? Are there gendered expectations? Or is there a more egalitarian approach that they might find acceptable?

James's situation is pretty common, as a lot of people find themselves attracted to someone who is just a little bit younger than they are. Figuring out what a person wants from a relationship may seem a little cold or clinical, but there are benefits to thinking in this linear fashion. First, it helped James think clearly about his situation: is sex with Janine worth a potential felony conviction? Next, it helped him think about his life beyond the passions of the moment; it is all too easy to decide something when we are feeling strong emotions, but a little clearheadedness goes a long way toward building a successful life. Finally, including Janine in the conversation is the best way for them to move forward, both as a couple and as individuals.

Analysis

James's approach to his potential relationship with Janine may feel a little clinical, but there are good reasons to be analytical about our relationships, especially if there are differences in age that could potentially lead to legal complications. There are age of consent laws in nearly every U.S. state, but there is a great deal of variability. For example, the age of consent in most states is sixteen, but it may allow for relationships between younger people depending on the age difference. In many states, relationships between people who are thirteen years old are acceptable, and people who are a couple of years older may also be able to have sex with thirteen-year-olds. There is so much variety in these consent laws that a person who is considering dating a person under the age of eighteen should check their state's laws regarding age of consent. In addition, the older person should also check in with their potential dating partner's parents; most cases of statutory rape (the name of the crime for people charged with sex with someone under the age of consent) are brought by parents appealing to law enforcement to prevent their child from engaging in future sexual activity.

The consequences of dating someone younger without checking age of consent laws and familiarizing oneself with the parents of the person you are interested in can be extreme. These cases can be prosecuted as either a misdemeanor or a felony, with more extreme punishments for felony statutory rape. According to the United States Sentencing Commission, the average jail time for a person convicted of statutory rape is thirty months.

Glossary

Asexual: Being asexual means that a person does not typically experience sexual attraction to others.

Bechdel test: The Bechdel test was developed by Allison Bechdel in her comic, *Dykes to Watch Out For* (1985). This test is a good measure of female agency in film and fiction and has three basic components: (1) does the film or fiction include at least two women; (2) do the two or more women have names; and (3) do the women who are named talk about something other than men?

Consent: Consent is the agreement to do something and is not inherently sexual. One can consent to a range of activities, from a cup of tea, to going to a movie, to engaging in sexual activity.

Cycle of abuse: The graphic image known as the cycle of abuse was first developed by Lenore E. Walker in the 1970s after she noticed patterns within abusive relationships.

Dating violence: Dating violence is any behavior that crosses a line between dating partners. This can include verbal abuse, including name-calling, shaming, or otherwise speaking negatively about one's partner; emotional abuse; and physical contact.

Domestic violence: Like dating violence, domestic violence is any behavior that crosses a line between intimate partners. There are at least three types of domestic violence: (1) verbal abuse, which includes belittling the partner, implying that they are not competent, or joking about their ditziness, especially in front of others; (2) emotional abuse, which frequently includes a verbal component but also includes neglect, giving their partner the cold shoulder, holding grudges against their partner for some perceived slight, or asking their partner to avoid certain people; and (3) physical abuse, which can include punching, kicking, slapping, poking their partner in their butt when they squat, inappropriate touching in public, and, at its worst, rape between two otherwise consensual intimate partners.

Gender: Gender is the socially constructed roles for men and women and typically leaves out people who are nonbinary.

HIPAA: HIPAA stands for the Health Insurance Portability and Accountability Act (1996) that federally mandates protection for patient's health information from being disclosed without their consent or knowledge.

Intersex: Intersex is a broad term to describe a variety of conditions in which the internal genitals and the external genitals do not match. Since this is a natural variation among humans, there is little reason to surgically or otherwise seek to fix the gender of intersex infants.

LGBTQIA+ community: The abbreviation LGBTQIA+ stands for lesbian, gay, bisexual, transgender, querying (or questioning their sexual identity), intersex, asexual, and more. It is a form of shorthand that helps people create an environment where everyone in a group can feel welcome. Many teachers use the abbreviation to invite students to be present as their authentic self, especially in the latter years of high school or college.

Media: Media is ubiquitous in the modern age, as we all have access to unlimited information, videos, chats, blogs, and social media to connect us to one another.

#MeToo: The #MeToo movement is a movement against sexual harassment, sexual abuse, and rape.

Nonbinary: Nonbinary is a category for people who do not fit neatly in the gender binary. This is also sometimes called gender fluid.

Perpetrator: A perpetrator is someone who is accused of having done something that is illegal. This can include dating or domestic violence, sexual harassment, sexual assault, and rape.

Pornography: Pornography is the production of images that are sexual in nature. It is intended for sexual titillation and frequently features the objectification and denigration of women.

PTSD: PTSD stands for post-traumatic stress disorder, and symptoms include flashbacks, nightmares, anxiety, and uncontrollable thoughts about the triggering event.

Rape: Rape is any sexual activity, typically involving penetration, without the full consent of one's partner. Consent can only be given if a person is fully cognizant of what they are doing, which means that people who are drunk or otherwise impaired are unable to consent.

Rape culture: Rape culture is the elements of our society that make it seem acceptable to sexualize other people against their will, leading to objectification, sexual assault, and rape.

Restraining order: A restraining order, sometimes also known as a protective order, is typically ordered by a victim and is granted or denied by a judge who deems that the victim is at risk for future abuse, whether physically or sexually.

Romeo and Juliet: The star-crossed lovers, Romeo and Juliet, are the titular characters in William Shakespeare's play (1597). The story focuses on the romance between the two characters but also the problem that their love creates as their families are currently feuding.

Sex offender registry: The sex offender registry, known in some places as Megan's Law, is a list of people who have been convicted of sexual-based crimes, including rape, child abuse or pedophilia, and sexual assault.

Sexual assault: Sexual assault is unwanted sexual touching that does not necessarily include penetration. This can include verbal assault through things like catcalling, whistling, or otherwise making a person feel uncomfortable or threatened by the behavior.

Sexuality: Sexuality refers to sexual feelings, thoughts, desires, and attraction toward others. You may find a person sexually, physically, or emotionally attractive.

SlutWalk: SlutWalks are organized to protest rape culture, including elements such as victim blaming and the slut-shaming of victims. The movement's goals are to reclaim the word *slut* as a term of empowerment and to undo the damage of rape culture's admonition that women should dress in a nonprovocative manner and that those who do not are rightly punished by sexual assault or rape.

Stalking and cyberstalking: Stalking is the tracking of a person's whereabouts and other activities without that person's knowledge or consent. Cyberstalking is tracking a person's on-line presence, or setting up alternate identities to check in on their target. Stalking is dangerous behavior which frequently ends negatively.

Statutory Rape: Statutory rape is the crime committed by those who have sex with people who are under their state's age of consent. Some states make allowances for people who begin their relationship prior to one person turning 18, called Romeo and Juliet laws; others deem sex between two people under their state's age of consent as a misdemeanor.

Transgender: Being transgender means that a person does not identify with the gender they were assigned at birth.

Directory of Resources

While many cities have local resources available through medical professionals or other caregivers, including teachers, counselors, and clergy, here is a list of nationwide resources that can be accessed for more information.

HOTLINES

National Domestic Violence Hotline: 1-800-799-SAFE (7233), https://www.thehotline.org

The National Domestic Violence Hotline: 1-800-799-7233 offers 24/7 support, information, and advocacy for people in dating or domestically violent situations. In addition to the hotline, an advocate will text with you if that is your preference and offer resources via the website: https://www.thehotline.org.

National Sexual Assault Hotline: 1-800-656-HOPE [4673], https://rainn.org/

This hotline is operated by the Rape, Abuse, and Incest National Network (RAINN). RAINN is the nation's largest anti-sexual violence advocate, and it operates the National Sexual Assault Hotline in partnership with over 1,000 local service providers. RAINN also operates the Department of Defense Safe Helpline for military who have been sexually assaulted or raped. Its website also offers a number of valuable resources.

National Teen Dating Violence Helpline: 1-866-331-9474, https://www
.loveisrespect.org/
> This helpline is operated by Love Is Respect. Love Is Respect offers
> resources for people experiencing dating or domestic violence, including
> information about dating, how to ask for consent, quizzes to help you
> determine whether your relationship is abusive, and how to set boundaries.

Trans Lifeline: 1-877-565-8860
> The Trans Lifeline is staffed by trans people and provide support for
> people in the trans community. In addition to providing this service,
> the trans lifeline also offers opportunities for trans people to work for
> the lifeline, as many trans folks have difficulty with employment.

WEBSITES AND NATIONAL ORGANIZATIONS

An Abuse, Rape, Domestic Violence Aid and Resource Center (AARD-
VARC): http://www.aardvarc.org/
> AARDVARC offers information for victims of dating violence, sexual
> assault, and rape.

Break the Silence against Domestic Violence (BTSADV): https://
breakthesilencedv.org
> BTSADV advocates for victims of dating and domestic violence.

DAWN: https://deafdawn.org/
> This site provides support for victims of dating or domestic violence,
> sexual abuse, and stalking who are deaf. While based in Washington,
> D.C., they provide referrals for deaf people throughout the U.S.

Fort Refuge: http://www.fortrefuge.com/
> Fort Refuge is an abuse survivors' website that offers support and
> resources, including quizzes and articles written by other survivors.

Human Rights Campaign (HRC): https://www.hrc.org/
> HRC offers information and support for people in the LGBTQIA+
> community, and it advocates for equality and respect, including fight-
> ing against anti-LGBTQIA+ laws.

Legal Dictionary: https://legaldictionary.net/romeo-and-juliet-laws/
> You can find information about Romeo and Juliet laws on the Legal
> Dictionary website. It offers a brief overview of what the laws are
> as well as the age of consent in all fifty states. Search here to learn

whether your state has such a law, what the age of consent is, and what age difference is acceptable before you begin a relationship with someone who is significantly older or younger than you.

National Center for Victims of Crime: https://victimsofcrime.org/
The National Center for Victims of Crime website is a one-stop shop for victims, professionals working with victims, and those who advocate on behalf of victims of crime, including a specific site for Washington, DC; a site for Native Americans who are victims of crime; and a site for victims of crime anywhere in the United States.

National Resource Center on Domestic Violence: https://www.nrcdv.org/
The National Resource Center on Domestic Violence is a one-stop shop for people who are experiencing domestic violence or those who wish to advocate for victims of domestic violence. There are numerous programs to support people who have experience domestic violence.

Pandora's Project: https://pandys.org/
Pandora's Project offers support for people who have experienced dating or domestic violence, sexual assault, harassment, or rape.

Planned Parenthood: https://www.plannedparenthood.org/
Planned Parenthood's website offers information about what to do after sexual assault and information about consent, birth control, sexually transmitted diseases, and other issues related to sexual health. Planned Parenthood is also supportive of people in the LGBTQIA+ community and offers information on determining sexual identity, sexual pleasure, and sexual orientation.

7 Cups: https://www.7cups.com/
This site offers free emotional support for people in the form of self-help guides, free 24/7 chat with caring listeners, and also offers affordable online therapy for $150 a month with licensed therapists.

Survivors Chat: http://www.survivorschat.com/
Survivors Chat gives survivors of incest, dating and domestic violence, sexual assault, harassment, and rape a chance to talk with other victims about their paths to well-being.

The Trevor Project: https://www.thetrevorproject.org
The Trevor Project provides support for people in the LGBTQIA+ community, works with researchers to reduce suicide rates, helps

allies and educators be more supportive, and advocates for a kinder world.

The Varying Age of Consent from State to State: https://www.dailydot .com/irl/age-of-consent-by-state/
    This resource provides the age of consent for the United States. This resource is useful for people who want to avoid charges of statutory rape.

BOOKS

Rape

Against Our Will: Men, Women, and Rape (1975), by Susan Brownmiller, is a foundational text considering rape and the ways in which it functions in our society. Brownmiller's text has helped many people see that rape is a part of American culture and has paved the way for feminists to think about the aspects of our culture that contribute to a rape culture.

I Never Called It Rape (1988), by Robin Warshaw, is one of the first texts to talk about the problem of date and acquaintance rape. Warshaw's text points out how people we already know are most frequently the ones who are most likely to rape us.

The Vagina Monologues (1996), by Eve Ensler is a play that explores women's relationships to their vaginas, including issues such as rape, periods, body image, reproductive, and prostitution through the eyes of numerous women.

CONSENT

Challenging Casanova: Beyond the Stereotype of the Promiscuous Young Male (2012), by Andrew P. Smiler, goes beyond the stereotype of young men as always ready for sex and instead claims that the type of masculinity explained by the Casanova Complex is the minority rather than the majority. This text also posits that erections do not imply consent, and it is LGBTQIA+ friendly.

Kisses, Condoms, and Consent (2021), by Will Decherd, is aimed at young adults, and it provides excellent advice for people just starting out with intimate relationships. Given that our culture typically does a poor job of preparing young people for intimate relationships, Decherd's book is a welcome addition for people who care about young adults and want to initiate conversations about consent.

Real Talk about Sex and Consent: What Every Teen Needs to Know (2020), by Cheryl M. Bradshaw, is similar to Popova's book. This text examines healthy boundary setting, coercion, reciprocity, and the importance of clear, honest communication. There is also information about sex and trauma, how pornography impacts our thinking about sexual behaviors, and cultural expectations regarding sexual activity.

Sexual Consent (2018), by Milena Popova, examines issues of sexual consent, feminism, and how consent works in real life, including how popular culture, including pornography, impacts our understanding of consent and asking for consent to sexual activity.

MOVIES

Many movies portray rape and dating violence, but few do the work of analyzing why these things continue to occur in our society. Here are a few titles that can help us think about our culture and the role that this violence plays.

The Accused (1988), which is based on a real rape case, follows the case of Sarah Tobias, a waitress who is gang-raped at a bar, as she works to ensure that her rapists and the men who encouraged them are prosecuted. While this is a fictionalized version of a real experience, it also looks at issues of classism, misogyny, post-traumatic stress disorder (PTSD), slut-shaming, victim blaming, and women's empowerment.

Dreamworlds 3: Desire, Sex, and Power (2007), a documentary by Sut Jhally, explores the dangerous obsession of music videos with violence and the objectification of women. While the film can be challenging to watch, the key takeaways make it worthwhile.

The Mask You Live In (2015), written, directed, and produced by Jennifer Seibel Newsom, explores the harmful ideas about masculinity in American culture and why violence is perceived to be normal or part of males being male.

Miss-Representation (2011) is similar to *The Mask You Live In* in that Jennifer Seibel Newsom analyzes the media's role in perpetuating sexist stereotypes that harm men and women. It is available for streaming online through numerous sources, including Amazon Prime.

Trevor (1997) is a short feature film directed by Peggy Rajski that follows the coming-out experience of a young man in the 1970s and his suicidal ideation. The film is important, as it became the catalyst for the Trevor Project, which provides mental health support for the LGBTQIA+ community.

Index

Adam Walsh Child Protection and
    Safety Act, 57
Addiction, 68
Alcohol, 20, 21, 40, 42, 50, 51, 58, 61,
    75, 77, 78, 87, 99, 107–108
  lowering of inhibitions, 31
  underage drinking, 18
  used to lure young people, 18
Anxiety, xxv, 5, 21, 30, 36, 42,
    46–47, 49–51, 68, 74, 76,
    107, 115
Apologies, 52, 77
Asexual, definition of, 113

Bechdel test, 65
  definition of, 113
Buddy system, 108
Bullying, 33, 36, 39, 40, 87, 90
Bush, George H. W., and Adam
    Walsh Child Protection and
    Safety Act, 57

Consent, xxiv, 4, 10–13, 15–18, 24,
    35–37, 55, 59–60, 62, 71, 80,

    87–89, 97, 102, 109, 111, 114,
    115, 116, 118, 119, 120
  definition of, 10, 113
  how to ask for it, 13, 65
  how to reply when asked, 12–13
  during sexual activity, xxiv, 4, 10,
    12, 15, 17, 36
Consequences of dating violence,
    xxiii, 3, 8, 23, 27, 31, 39, 46,
    51, 53, 60, 63, 64, 69, 78, 79,
    85
Consequences of domestic violence,
    xiii, xiv, 4, 7–8, 9, 31–32,
    33–34, 37, 39–41, 45, 48–49,
    52, 54, 55, 65, 67–68, 70, 71,
    72, 73, 79, 81, 82, 83
Consequences of rape, 41
  mental effects of, 32, 40, 42
  pregnancy, 11, 26, 39, 41, 44
  sexually transmitted diseases, 41
  social network, 43, 45
Consequences of sexual assault, 51,
    53, 58
Cyberbullying, 6, 67

Cyberstalking, 4, 6, 26–27, 33, 116
Cycle of abuse, 9, 37–39
    definition of, 113

Dating violence, xxiii–xxv, 3–23,
    27, 51, 53, 60, 63, 64, 69,
    78–79, 81, 85
    causes, 31–34
    and consent, 10–13
    consequences of, 39–41
    definition of, 113
    prevalence of, 6–8
    psychological effects, 46–48
    signs of, 8–10
Depression, 5, 21, 30, 40, 42, 46, 47,
    50, 51, 68, 107
*Diagnostic and Statistical Manual of
    Mental Disorders* (DSM), 49,
    50, 104
Dissociation, 5, 21, 42, 46, 48, 68
Domestic violence, xiii–xxiv, 4, 7–9,
    31–32, 33–34, 37, 39, 40, 41,
    45, 48, 49, 52, 54–55, 65, 67, 68
    definition of, 114

Eating disorders, 40, 42–43, 45, 46,
    47, 68
Eye movement desensitization and
    reprocessing therapy, 50, 68

False charges of rape/dating violence,
    27–30
Fight, flight, or freeze, 22, 48, 49
Fraternities, 41, 86, 87

Gender, definition of, 114

Harassment, 4, 33, 35, 54, 67, 71,
    82–83, 88, 91, 93, 103, 104,
    114, 115, 119
Hate crimes, 67, 70
Healthy relationships, 9, 10, 11, 13,
    32–33, 36, 40–41, 44–45, 50,
    69, 70–71, 80, 105, 109, 120

HIPAA (Health Insurance Portability
    and Accountability Act),
    76, 107
    definition of, 114

International Megan's Law to Prevent
    Child Exploitation and
    Other Sexual Crimes through
    Advance Notification of
    Traveling Sex Offenders,
    57–58
Intersex, definition of, 114
Intimate partner violence, xxiv, 3,
    6–8, 17, 20–21, 25–26, 32–33,
    35, 42–43, 45, 72, 75, 78,
    81–82, 103–104, 114
    stranger danger, 17, 22, 60, 73, 90
    victim-blaming, 9, 36, 89–90,
    116, 121

Legal system, 14–16, 24, 41
    district attorneys, 20, 29, 34
    police investigations, 28, 85
LGBTQIA+, xiii, 6, 9, 20, 34–36,
    51–53, 56, 68, 69, 70, 71, 72,
    88, 94, 114, 118, 119, 120, 121
    dead-naming, 104
    discrimination against, 71, 103
    legal system, 70–71, 103
    medical care, 102–103
LGBTQIA+ community, definition
    of, 114

Mandated reporters, 81
Media
    definition of, 114
    impact of, 85–87
Megan's Law, 57
#MeToo movement, xiii, 28, 91–93
    definition of, 114
Military, 15, 20, 43, 48, 51, 71,
    79, 117

Nonbinary, definition of, 115

Obama, Barack, and the International Megan's Law to Prevent Child Exploitation and Other Sexual Crimes through Advance Notification of Traveling Sex Offenders, 57

Perpetrator(s)
  consequences, legal, 53–55
  conviction, impact on life, 58–60
  definition of, 115
  psychological impacts of, 51–53
Pornography, definition of, 115
Post-traumatic stress disorder (PTSD), xxv, 42, 45, 46, 48–51, 68, 74, 76, 115
  chronic PTSD, 46
  symptoms of, 40, 48
  treatments for, 49–51
Pornography, 17, 52, 58, 115, 120
  rape as feature of, 86, 88–89
Post-coital regret, 30, 90
Pregnancy, 41, 71
  complications of, 44
  emergency contraception, 44, 108
  myths, 14
  teen pregnancies, 56
  as a weapon of war, 26
Prevention of, rape and dating violence, 60–64
Psychological effects, long-term, 46–48
Psychotherapy, 39, 50, 54, 68, 74–76, 78, 119
PTSD (post-traumatic stress disorder), xxv, 42, 45, 46, 48–51, 68, 74, 76
  chronic PTSD, 46
  definition of, 115
  symptoms of, 40, 48
  treatments for, 49–51

Rape, 13–15, 17, 18, 34, 51, 53, 57, 58, 60, 64, 67, 76, 81
  actions following, 18–19, 73–76
  and alcohol, 18, 20, 21, 31, 40, 42, 50–51, 58, 61, 75, 77–78, 87, 99, 107–108
  causes, 34–37
  consequences of, 41–43
  definition of, 13, 115
  false charges of, 27–30, 88
  LGBTQIA+ community and, 6, 9–10, 20, 34–36, 52–53, 68, 70–71, 72, 88, 94, 114, 118, 119, 120, 121
  men as victims of rape, xxiii–xxiv, 18–21, 29, 52
  pregnancy as a result of, 26, 39, 43–46, 71, 108
  psychological effects, 46–48
  sexual assault and, xiii, 11–12, 14, 17–20, 28–29, 32, 42, 46–48, 51, 53–55, 58–66, 67–73, 75–77, 88–94, 104, 109, 115–120
  signs of, 21–23
  statutory rape, 15–17, 79–81
  teaching women how to avoid, 22, 35, 37, 63–64, 89
Rape culture, xiii, 34–36, 52, 65–66, 85–91, 94, 116, 120
  boys will be boys attitude, 88
  catcalling, 17, 25, 35, 65, 88, 116
  definition of, 115
  gender norms and, 35, 86, 88, 103
  pornography, 17, 27, 33, 52, 58, 86, 88, 89, 115
  rape jokes, 65, 87–88, 90
  slut-shaming, 43, 87–88, 90, 94–95, 116
  victim-blaming, 9, 36–37, 43, 87, 89–90, 116, 121
Restraining orders, 41, 54, 64, 70, 82–83, 106
  definition of, 115
  gun ownership and, 54, 55, 79, 83
Romeo and Juliet laws, 55–57, 80, 109
Romeo and Juliet, definition of, 115

Self-harm, 40, 50, 68
Services for
    victims of dating violence, 69–73
    victims of rape and sexual assault,
        67–69
Sex offender's registry (list), xxv,
        15–16, 18, 41, 53, 55–56,
        57–58, 59, 68, 79–80, 91
    definition of, 115
Sexual assault, xiii, 11–12, 14, 17–20,
        28–29, 32, 42, 46–48, 51,
        53–55, 58–66, 67–73, 75–77,
        88–94, 104, 109
    definition of, 115–116
Sexual harassment, 4, 33, 35, 54, 67,
        71, 82–83, 88, 91, 93, 103,
        104, 114, 115, 119
Sexuality, definition of, 116
SlutWalks, 63, 93–95
    definition of, 116
    organizing, 63, 93–95, 116
    origins, 94
Social media, 4, 6, 27, 33, 43, 58, 62,
        64, 87, 90, 95, 114

Sororities, 41, 86, 87
Stalking, xxiv, 4–6, 20–21, 26–27,
        32, 33–34, 54, 64, 67, 82–83,
        106, 118
    definition of, 116
Statutory rape, 15–17, 79
    definition of, 116
Suicidal ideation, 21, 40, 50, 56, 68,
        99, 101, 106, 119, 121

Toxic masculinity, 36, 65
Transgender, definition of, 116

United Nations International
        Children's Emergency Fund
        (UNICEF), 22

Vagina Monologues, xiv,
        120
Victim blaming, 9, 36–37, 43, 87,
        89–90, 116, 121

Walker, Lenore E., and cycle of abuse
        concept, 37

About the Author

Lee A. Ritscher, PhD, teaches at California State University Monterey Bay and at Hartnell College. Her book, *The Semiotics of Rape in Renaissance English Literature* (2009), explores the ways in which legal theory and flawed medical thinking worked together to coerce rape victims into silence. She received her bachelor's degree from Tennessee State University, her master's degree from the University of Notre Dame, and her PhD from the University of California Santa Cruz.